AELRED OF
RIEVAULX

D0880280

AELRED OF RIEVAULX

The Way of Friendship

selected spiritual writings

introduced and edited by
M. Basil Pennington

New City Press

To
the Novices
of
Assumption Abbey
who are discovering the
Way of Frienship

Published in the United States by New City Press
202 Cardinal Rd., Hyde Park, NY 12538
©2001 New City Press

Cover design by Nick Cianfarani

Library of Congress Cataloging-in-Publication Data:
Aelred, of Rievaulx, Saint, 1110-1167.
The way of friendship : selected spiritual writings / Aelred of Rievaulx ; introduced and
edited by M. Basil Pennington.
        p.   cm.
    ISBN 1-56548-128-3
    1. Spiritual life--Catholic Church--early works to 1800.   2. Friendship--Religious
aspects--Christianity--Early works to 1800.   3. Catholic Church—Doctrine--Early works
to 1800.   I. Pennington, M. Basil.   II. Title.

BX2349 .A47   2000
241'.6762—dc21   00-060943

Printed in Canada

Contents

Welcome

Aelred of Rievaulx has gained a new popularity in our times for he is a man of our times: an introspective man of love, a full-blooded humanist, who understood and spoke clearly of human psychology. He knew by experience all the yearnings of the human heart. He was not afraid to experience and speak out of his experience. He was fully human, a man who knew that the human heart longed for something more than all the rich joys of human friendships. He dared to speak of, long for and enter into friendship with the Divine, to find his fulfillment there. And he pointed his sons, his friends and us in that direction in very practical ways. He helps us sort out the emotions of the human heart, acknowledging all their goodness, placing them in the context where they can lead to or give way to a fuller human fulfillment and happiness.

Aelred's romanticism, if you want to call it that, is grounded in solid theology and psychology. It is not by chance that he first worked out a complete and very existential ascetical and mystical theology in his basic work, *The Mirror of Charity*. The Cistercians, whose whole reform was geared toward living the gospels according to the practical wisdom of Benedict of Nursia's *Rule for Monasteries*, saw the "school of the Lord's service" as meant to blossom into the "school of love," the *schola caritatis*. Using a Pauline image popular in his century, Aelred will produce a pastoral text that would mirror—therefore show in a full but limited way—the way of love, human and divine, to which we are all called as the only way to true happiness and fulfillment. It is such a basic and essential way that what he writes is readily applicable to every Christian life. It is on this solid foundation that he continues his pastoral guidance in his very existential tripartite explanation of *Spiritual Friendship*. He does present some accompanying tones in his less important pieces. *Jesus at the Age of Twelve* fills out the humanism. The *Rule,* written for his sister, makes it clear that he writes for women as well as for men. His *Geneology of the Kings* and *Battle of the Standard* show he was very much aware of the currents of history, of the evolution of human consciousness and theological insights, and of the applicability of basic spirituality—the ways the human responds to the call to enter into the Divine—to men and women of every social standing, men and women very much in the world.

Aelred was born in 1110 at the very time the master of the Cistercian School, Bernard of Fontaines (later of Clairvaux) was preparing to enter upon the Cistercian way. Born into a curious family—his father was the last married priest to minister at the shrine of the saints at Hexham in what is today southeast Scotland—he experienced a curious upbringing. At an early age he was transplanted to the court of the King of Scotland, the saintly King David. There he grew up as an intimate companion not only of the crown prince, Henry, but also of Waldef, one of the king's two stepsons. This saintly man preceded Aelred to the religious life, joining the Canons, but he would eventually follow Aelred in embracing the Cistercian way.

Much in line with the piety of his time, Aelred later spoke of his sinful adolescence in way that invites our imagination to conceive of all sorts of excesses. But the fact is, he evidently was considered a rather pious young man and was steered toward the cloister, which he entered at twenty-four. Before entering, like most of the Cistercian Fathers, he acquired a good classical and literary education as is evidenced by his later writings. The court must have had some good tutors. The young man's appointment as the court's major-domo shows him to be a dutiful young man, who didn't mind attending to the details while the others ate and drank and made merry.

An idealism which never abandoned him drew him to the White Monks, who were just then expanding into the British Isles, an expansion Aelred would greatly foster. One of the fundamental challenges of every human life is to cope with idealism and realism. We can cling to some idealistic image of the way human life should be and spin around unsettled all our life. Or we can give up our ideals and settle in the "real" and live a rather disappointing or maybe even a profoundly disappointed life. Or we can choose to live in the dynamic and exciting tension of a life that clings to an ideal, lovingly embraces the real—in oneself and in others and in all else—and gently moves toward the ideal. Though in some respects Aelred failed in gentleness toward himself and ruined his health, he fully lived this kind of exciting life, and it was this that attracted so many to him and still attracts us to him today. He portrays an ideal of friendship, human and divine, that speaks to the deepest and loftiest ideals of our hearts. He most compassionately draws a picture that embraces the real humanness we all experience, rejects none of it, and shows how it can be the coinage to purchase the ideal for which we long. How could a man who in the last weeks of his life could pen a treatise *On the Soul* not have lots of soul?

In this slim volume we will let Aelred help us lay some solid foundations through *The Mirror of Charity* and walk with him in the exciting way of *Spiritual Friendship*. This will be enriched by some of the teaching he gave in his many sermons, some of his prayers and words of life. A brief anthology can do little more than offer a taste. A bibliography will indicate where Aelred's writings can be found in their entirety as well as deep and beautiful studies of this beautiful man of God and man of man and woman.

Aelred became a monk at twenty-four, an abbot and spiritual father in full sense at thirty-three, at first the abbot of Revesby and then of Rievaulx, and he lived that vocation for over twenty years. In one of his most beautiful published prayers he allows us to overhear the hopes and aspirations he lived in those years of self-giving ministry. Here more than anywhere else will the reader want to go in quest of the full text. Rightly we honor this blessed man on the day of his passing, January 12, and though many centuries have passed since 1167 we continue to ask his pastoral care. Fifty-seven seems quite young to us today, but it was a venerable age in a time when the average male longevity was forty. Aelred's later years were marked by a terrible painful debilitating arthritis. He certainly can inspire us senior citizens of today in the way he continued to be so lovingly present to the young so that they flocked to him, crowded his room, sat on his bed and all about it, happy to spend some time in his heart-warming presence. We can learn from our dear abbot some of the secrets of a rich and full old age.

Aelred has become popular with the gay community in our times, along with David, who loved his friend Jonathan "above the love of women." It is not surprising, for our troubadour of friendship speaks only of his friendships with men and this with much beauty and sensitivity. He entered the monastery at a fairly early age and lived his life almost exclusively in the company of men. Nonetheless, he speaks unambiguously about homosexual activity: ". . . that abominable sin which inflames a man with passion for a man. . . ."

Translations

The translations used here are taken for the most part from *The Works of Aelred of Rievaulx*, published by Cistercian Publications (Kalamazoo, Michigan) in the "Cistercian Fathers Series." However, I have not hesitated to revise them when I felt Aelred's Latin could be better expressed. I am grateful to all the translators and editors of Cistercian Publications, who have been working with me these past thirty years to make the extensive corpus of Cistercian patristic writings available in English. The labor is far from finished.

M. Basil Pennington, o.c.s.o.

True Charity

This very sensitive and even passionate young man of thirty-two, in a classical style still popular in his time, claims inadequacy for the task that was laid upon him: to give us a *Mirror of Charity*. But there can be no doubt that he was in truth a brilliant, gifted and highly respected young monk. Indeed, of all the monks and canons of Yorkshire he was the one chosen to represent the superiors of the region before the pope at Rome. Coming to his literary endeavor he brings together a rich lived experience of human life at court and in the monastery, a classical formation which he displays and eight years of monastic formation under a master chosen by Bernard of Clairvaux, Bernard's own secretary, the saintly William. Aelred's *Mirror* is not a speculative work but a very practical one, because not only did this passionate young man still need to assimilate the rich Cistercian spirituality himself, but he was now charged as novice master to help others, many others in the crowded novitiate of Rievaulx, to do the same. His *Mirror* was for them and for novices throughout the rapidly expanding order.

Although Aelred has not frankly told us, as did William of Saint Thierry when he wrote his *Meditations* "to help the young learn how to pray," this work was undoubtedly the fruit of gathering together notes made in the course of his monastic years. It brings together a number of literary forms: the dialogue he will use so effectively in his sequel on spiritual friendship; prayers which will in time be all drawn up into this masterful Pastoral Prayer; succinct argumentation and exposition; soliloquy and a passionately beautiful lament. It is in fact a quite extensive work, which later saw many popular summaries drawn from its abundance of practical wisdom. And yet it is so clearly one. Love is the frame, love silvers the glass, so that all, from the first moment of creation to the fullness of the eternal Sabbath, is framed by love and reflected in love.

The Way of Love

Let your voice sound in my ears, good Jesus, so that my heart may learn how to love you, my mind how to love you, the inmost being of my soul how to love you. Let the inmost core of my heart embrace you, my one and only true good, my dear and delightful joy. But, my God, what is love? Unless I am mistaken, love is a wonderful delight of the spirit: all the more attractive because more chaste, all the more gentle because more guileless, and all the more enjoyable because more ample. It is the heart's palate which tastes that you are sweet, the heart's eye which sees that you are good. The heart is the place capable of receiving you, great as you are. Someone who loves you grasps you. The more one loves the more one grasps, because you yourself are love, you are charity. This is the abundance of your house, by which your beloved will become so inebriated that, quitting himself or herself, this one will pass into you. And how else, O Lord, but by loving you and this with all one's being.

I pray you, Lord, let but a drop of your surpassing sweetness fall upon my soul, that by it the bread of my bitterness may become sweet. In experiencing a drop of this, may I have a foretaste of what to desire, what to long for, what to sigh for here on my pilgrimage. In my hunger let me have a foretaste, in my thirst let me drink. For those who eat you will still hunger, and those who drink you will still thirst. Yet they shall be filled when your glory appears and when will be manifest the abundance of your sweetness, which you reserve for those who fear you, and disclose only to those who love you.

Meanwhile I shall seek you, O Lord, seek you by loving you. One who advances on the way loving you, O Lord, surely seeks you. And one who loves you perfectly, O Lord, is one who has already found you. And what is more equitable than that your creature should love you, since from you it received the ability to love you? Creatures without reason or without sensation cannot love you; that is not their way. Of course, they also have their own way, their beauty and their order. Not that thereby they are or can be happy by loving you but that thereby, thanks to you, by their goodness, form and order they may advance the glory of those creatures who can be happy because they can love you.

(*Mirror of Charity* 1:2-3)

God's Creation

Now our God, whose being is supreme and unchangeable, whose being is ever the same (as David says: You are ever the same) has allotted to all his creatures these three gifts in common: nature, form and usefulness; a nature by which all are good, a form by which all are beautiful, and usefulness by which all in good order may serve some purpose. He who is responsible for their being is also responsible for their being good, beautiful, and well ordered. They all exist, because they are from him who is supreme and unchangeable being. All are beautiful, because they are from him who is supremely and unchangeably beautiful. All are good, because they are from him who is supremely and unchangeably good. All are well ordered, because they are from him who is supremely and unchangeably wise. They are therefore good by nature, beautiful in form, and well ordered that they might give splendor to the universe itself.

God saw all things he had made, it says, and they were very good. In as far as they exist, then, they are good. In as far as each part is in harmony with its entirety, they are beautiful. In as far as each thing in the universe keeps its proper place, time, and measure, all are in excellent order. Thus everything has a fitting place in which to exist: For example, angels have

heaven, irrational beings have earth, and humans have paradise, which is midway. In the same way each has its specific
time and duration. For example, in the beauty of the universe
one being, like the angelic nature, begins all at once but never
ends. Others, like human beings, although they do not all
begin together, nevertheless once begun they will not cease to
exist. Still others like irrational beings do not begin together
and at some time or other cease to exist. . . .

We must now turn our attention to the Creator's wisdom
and proclaim it. Although he is not the Creator or Abettor of
evils, nevertheless he rules over these evils with the utmost
prudence. Why, then, should my most gentle and at the same
time most mighty Lord not allow evil to exist, since evil cannot
overthrow his eternal plan in the slightest way? What, moreover, could make his own power appear more manifest, his
wisdom more awesome, his mercy more tender than that he
can omnipotently bring good out of evil, wisely keep in order
what has been set in order, and mercifully confer happiness on
the miserable?

(*Mirror of Charity* 1:4-7)

Our Beatitude

In creating the universe, then, God gave us not only being,
and not only some good or beautiful or well-ordered being, as
God did with other creatures, but in addition God granted
that we be happy. But as no creature has being of itself nor is
any beautiful or good of itself but from God who is the
supreme Being, supremely Good and Beautiful and therefore
the Goodness of all things good, the Beauty of all things beautiful and the Cause of all existent things, so a creature is not
happy of itself but from the One who is supremely happy and
therefore the Happiness of all the blessed.

Only a rational creature is capable of this happiness. Made in the image of its Creator, this creature is fitted to cling to the Creator whose image it is, because this is the rational creature's sole good. As Saint David says: For me to cling to God is good. Obviously this clinging is not of the flesh but of the spirit, since the author of all natures inserted in this creature three things that allow it to share God's eternity, participate in God's wisdom and taste God's sweetness. By these three I mean memory, understanding and love or will. Memory is capable of sharing God's eternity, understanding God's wisdom and love God's sweetness. By these three the first man was fashioned in the image of the Trinity; his memory held fast to God without forgetfulness, his understanding recognized God without error, and his love embraced God without a self-centered desire for anything else. And so this man was happy.

Although happiness is achieved in or through all three, still the taste of happiness is proper to the third. How very miserable it would be to be delighted with what is worst, where indeed there is neither delight nor any happiness. Again, where there is no love, there is no delight. Finally, the greater the love for the highest good, the greater the delight and the greater the happiness. Though memory may bring forth many things and knowledge grasp deep things, unless the will itself turns to what is presented or grasped, there is still no delight.

(*Mirror of Charity* 1:8-10)

The Fall

Our first parent was endowed with free will and aided by God's grace. By a lasting love of God, he could, without it ever ending, have taken delight in the memory and knowledge of God and been everlastingly happy. But he could also divert his love to something less, and so by withdrawing from God's love begin to grow cold and deliver himself up to misery. Now for a rational creature, just as there is no other happiness than to cling to God, so its misery is to withdraw from God. But set in honor, this man did not understand. Understand what? Perhaps what one said upon entering God's sanctuary and understanding truths not only about the present but also about the last day: "Those who withdraw from you will perish; you destroyed all adulterous betrayers." He did not understand that those who by pride betray God stumble into foolishness, and that anyone who by theft usurps the likeness of God is rightly garbed in the unlikeness of beasts.

By abusing free choice, then, the first man diverted his love from that changeless good and, blinded by his own self-centeredness, he directed his love to what was inferior. Thus withdrawing from the true good and deviating toward what of itself was not good, where he anticipated gain he found loss. By perversely loving himself he lost both himself and God. Thus it very justly came about that someone who sought the likeness of God in defiance of God, the more he wanted to become similar to God out of curiosity, the more dissimilar he became through self-centeredness. Therefore, the image of God became disfigured in us without becoming wholly destroyed. Consequently we have memory, but it is subject to forgetfulness; understanding, but it is open to error; and love, but it is prone to self-centeredness.

In this trinity within the rational soul there still persists an imprint, however faint, of the blessed Trinity. It was stamped on the very substance of the soul, for the soul remembers itself, knows itself and loves itself. The soul loves, knows and remembers the very memory of itself; remembers, knows and loves the very knowledge of itself; and likewise loves, remembers and knows its own love of itself. The soul then mirrors the Unity in its substance and the Trinity in the three words we have woven together. Accordingly, the psalmist says: "Surely the human person passes by in an image but is troubled in vain." By these words holy David suggests briefly but quite explicitly that the human soul does not lack the image by

nature and that its disfigurement comes from sin. Indeed,
forgetfulness distorts memory, error clouds knowledge, and
self-centeredness stifles love.

(*Mirror of Charity* 1:11-13)

Restoration in Christ

Through Jesus Christ, the mediator between God and us,
the debt for which human nature was being held liable had at
last been paid, and the contract by which our ancient enemy
with menacing pride held us bound had been destroyed. The
principalities and powers to whom divine justice had
submitted us had been despoiled. God the Father had finally
been appeased by that unique Victim on the cross. Then
memory is restored by the words of sacred scripture, understanding by the mystery of faith, and love by the daily increase
of charity. The restoration of the image will be complete if no
forgetfulness falsifies memory, if no error clouds our knowledge, and no self-centeredness claims our love. But where will
that be and when? This peace, this tranquillity, this felicity
may be hoped for in our homeland, where there is no opportu-
nity for forgetfulness among those living in eternity, nor any
creeping in of error among those enjoying the truth, nor any
impulse of self-centeredness among those absorbed in divine
charity. O charity eternal and true! O eternity true and
beloved! O truth beloved and eternal! O Trinity, eternal, true
and beloved! There, there is rest, there peace, there happy
tranquillity! There is tranquil happiness, there happy and
tranquil joyfulness.

(*Mirror of Charity* 1:14)

Life in This World

What are you doing, O human soul, what are you doing? Why are you seized by so many distractions? One thing alone is necessary. Why so many? Whatever you seek in the many exists in the one. If you long for excellence, knowledge, delight, abundance, all is there, there to perfection and nowhere else but there. Can real excellence exist in this swamp of misery and miry bog? Or perfect knowledge in this realm of the shadow of death? Or real delight in this place of horror and vast solitude? Or genuine abundance amid so many hardships? Again, in this world, what excellence exists which fear does not overthrow? How great is man's knowledge when he does not even grasp himself? If you delight in the flesh, so do the horse and the mule, which have no understanding. If you delight in glory or wealth, you will not take it with you when you die nor will your glory go with you. Real excellence exists where there is nothing higher to strive for, real knowledge exists where nothing remains unknown. That delight is real which is not lessened by boredom, and that abundance is real which is never exhausted. Woe to us, Lord, because we have withdrawn from you! Alas for me, that my stay has been prolonged. When shall I come and appear before your face? Who will give me the wings of a dove that I may fly away and be at rest?

Meanwhile let my soul grow wings, Lord Jesus; I ask, let my soul grow wings in the nest of your discipline. Let it rest in the clefts of the rock, in the hollow of the wall. Let my soul meanwhile embrace you crucified and take a drought of your precious blood. Let this sweet meditation meanwhile fill my memory, lest forgetfulness wholly darken it. Let me meanwhile judge that I know nothing but my Lord and him crucified, lest empty error lure my knowledge from the firm ground of faith. May your wondrous love claim all my love for itself, lest worldly self-centeredness engulf it. What then? Do I hope for this for myself alone? Fulfill, I ask you, Lord, fulfill that prophecy: "All the ends of the earth will remember and turn back to the Lord." They will remember, it says. It means that in a rational mind the memory of God is concealed, not utterly buried, so that it is not so much something newly engrafted but an old truth restored. For unless human reason did not gleam naturally in some way, even just a little, with the memory of God, I think there would be no reason why the fool would say in his heart, there is no God.

(Mirror of Charity 1:15-16)

Restoration through Charity

It is obvious, if I am not mistaken, that just as human pride, by departing from the supreme good not by a footstep but by the mind's attachment and becoming decrepit in itself, disfigured God's image in itself, so human humility, by approaching God by the spirit's attachment, is restored to the image of the Creator. Hence the apostle says: "Be renewed in the spirit of your mind and put on the new man, who was created according to God." But how will this renewal come about except by the new precept of charity of which the Savior says: "I give you a new commandment." Then, if the mind puts on this charity perfectly, charity will straightway reform the other two, namely, memory and knowledge, which we said were equally disfigured. A summary of this one precept, then, is presented to us in a very salutary way; it contains the divesting of the old man, the renewal of his mind and the reforming of the divine image.

(Mirror of Charity 1:24)

The Struggle of Love

Since only that power of the soul which is more usually called love is capable both of charity and of self-centeredness, this love is obviously divided against itself, as if by opposing appetites caused by the new infusion of charity and the remnants of a decrepit self-centeredness. About this the apostle says: "I do not do what I will," and again: "The flesh lusts against the spirit and the spirit against the flesh." These are so mutually opposed that you do not do the very things you will. Understand that, contrary to what the corrupt Manichaeans foolishly say, by the terms spirit and flesh, the apostle in no way describes two opposing natures in one person. By the word spirit, he expressed rather the renewal of the mind caused by the infusion of charity, for the love of God has been poured into out hearts by the Holy Spirit, who has been given to us. By the word flesh, he suggests the wretched slavery of the soul caused by the remnants of decrepitude. He affirms that an unending conflict rises in the one mind between an old familiar state and a new and unfamiliar one.

(Mirror of Charity 1:27)

The Sublimity of Divine Charity

The number seven was reserved for God's rest. God's rest we called his charity. Rightly so. "The Father loves the Son," scripture says, and shows him all that he does. And again: "As I keep my Father's commandments, so I remain in his good pleasure." And the Father testifies: "This is my beloved Son, in whom I am well pleased." This mutual delight of Father and Son is the gentlest love, the pleasing embrace and the most blessed charity by which the Father reposes in his Son and the Son in his Father. This imperturbable rest, genuine peace, eternal calm, incomparable goodness and indivisible unity is

surely the unity of both, or rather, that in which each possesses
the unity, sweetness, kindness and joy we call Holy Spirit. It is
for this reason that he is believed to have assumed this title as
properly his own, because it is clearly common to both.

Now although each of the two, Father and Son, is Spirit and
each is holy, still he who proceeds from both, namely the
consubstantial charity and unity of both, is properly called
Holy Spirit. Though he is one person and one being with the
Father and the Son, still because of the sevenfold grace which
is believed to flow from the fullness of that fountain, he is
referred to in scripture by the number seven. Hence also,
according to Zechariah, on one stone are discovered seven
eyes. And according to the Apocalypse, seven spirits stand
before the throne of God. You see, then, how great is the excellence of charity, in which the Creator and Ruler of all things
celebrates an unending and ineffable Sabbath.

Moreover, if you more closely contemplate every creature,
from the first to the last, from the highest to the lowest, from
the loftiest angel to the lowliest worm, you will surely discover
divine goodness—which we have called nothing other than
divine charity. It contains, enfolds and penetrates all things,
not by pouring into a place or being diffused in space or by
nimbly moving about but by the steady, mysterious and
self-contained simplicity of its substantial presence. Charity
joins the lowest to the highest, binds in harmonious peace
contraries to contraries, cold to hot, wet to dry, smooth to
rough, hard to soft, so that among all creatures there can be
nothing adverse, nothing contradictory, nothing unbecoming,
nothing disturbing, nothing to disfigure the beauty of the
universe. All things should rest, as it were, in utterly tranquil
peace, with the tranquillity of that order which charity
ordained for the universe. Hence anything which bursts its
bonds and goes beyond the order of divine goodness is soon
caught up by the order of that supremely unconquered power.
So although in itself this thing may be restless and disordered,
not only is it not a hindrance to the tranquillity of the unwise

but it is a great help, if only by comparison with it beautiful things are judged to be more beautiful and good things better.

(Mirror of Charity 1:57-59)

The Quest for Happiness

This privilege of rising above the physical senses to strive for higher things is reserved for you, O rational soul, in preference to other living things. You will never satisfy your desire until by a felicitous curiosity you reach what is highest and best, what nothing surpasses and nothing excels. Wherever you stand below that, however high or great or pleasant it may be adjudged, you will doubtlessly remain miserable. Miserable, because needy. Needy, because ahead lies what you seek; ahead lies what you are panting for; ahead lies that happiness toward the achievement of which a natural force drives the rational soul. Since the conscience of each and every individual testifies that all humans want to be happy and since this will can in no way be destroyed, obviously a rational creature can attain the rest desired by all humans only by attaining happiness.

The blind perversity of us miserable humans is lamentable. Although we desire happiness ardently, not only do we not do those things by which we may obtain our desire but rather, with contrary disaffection, we take steps to add to our misery. In my opinion, we would never do this if a false image of happiness were not deceiving us or a semblance of real misery frightening us off from happiness. Is there anyone who does not see that poverty, grief, hunger and thirst are no slight part of our misery? Yet through them real misery is frequently averted and eternal happiness pursued. Blessed are you poor, said Jesus, for yours is the kingdom of heaven. Blessed are you who weep, for you shall he comforted. Blessed are you who hunger now, for you shall he satisfied. Poverty, then is rewarded with eternal riches, grief is changed to eternal joy, for the hungry eternal satisfaction is in store. There is no one who doubts that all these: riches, joy and satisfaction are not lacking in happiness. But because an appearance of joy deludes any wicked person by some attachment of his will, his false delight disappears with the satisfaction of his desires, while in his misery he does not know what consolation there is for the elect even in oppression and what rejoicing in hope.

The wicked dread an unhappy face. But under the hue of happiness one grasps at real unhappiness, the false joy which does not escape real sorrow, preferring that to the misery which presages true happiness. Such a one is like a sick person who earnestly hopes to recover but because of the immediate pain shuns an amputation or dreads cauterization. Lured by immediate relief the sick one demands the fomentation of an oil poultice, although the disease is such that it rages more with this gentle treatment and would not with the pain of cautery or amputation. So a person is miserable and deceived as long as such a one thinks that happiness is something it is not or is allured by the agreeableness of things that are deceptive. We get used to misery and, indeed, never lose our longing for happiness. As if struggling unhappily in a circle, we never rest. Now since God alone is superior and an angel equal to a rational soul and all other things are considered inferior, what is closer to madness than to abandon the superior and to pine for rest in beings inferior to oneself?

(*Mirror of Charity* 1:62-64)

Where Human Happiness Will Not Be Found

O wondrous creature, inferior only to the Creator, how much will you debase yourself? Do you love the world? But you yourself are superior to the world. Do you admire the sun?

But you yourself are brighter than the sun. Do you philoso-
phize about the harmony of the revolving heavens? But you
are more sublime than the heavens. Do you examine the
mysterious causes of creation? But no creature is a greater
mystery than you. Do you doubt it, when you may pass judgment on all creatures, yet none of them on you? But if you
wish to judge them, then do not love them. Do not love to
judge them. Love the Creator who set you over, not under, all
creatures. The Creator set you over them not that through
them you might be happier but that the Creator might be the
one through whom you would be superior, subjecting all
things to you as a crowning honor and keeping Godself for you
as rewarding happiness. Why then do you pursue fleeting
beauties, when your own beauty neither fades with age nor
grows shabby with poverty nor becomes wan with illness nor is
ruined even by death itself? Seek what you seek but not there.
You are seeking that nothing may elude your will and that thus
you may find rest. Then seek this. Where, you ask? Not in
health of the body. For if you love it so much that you seek rest
there, realize with what efforts you acquire it if you do not
have it, and with what painful remedies painful diseases are
driven out. If you enjoy good health, consider how much care
is required to maintain it. And how many diseases, fevers,
plagues and finally death lie in wait for it!

What then? Is it in wealth? But what a task to acquire it,
what anxiety to keep it, what dread lest it be lost, what grief if
it slips away. You increase your money only to increase your
anxiety. You fear the powerful may extort it. You fear a thief
may steal it. You fear a clerk may lose it. Who can say how
often happens what the wise man describes: "Riches were
stored up to their owner's loss." The poor man, therefore, rests
more easily. The traveler with empty pockets—as someone
said—does not fear the robber's ambush. With his gate
unbarred, the poor man sleeps safe from nocturnal burglars.
The satirist's verse says the same: The traveler with pockets
empty whistles in the face of the highwayman.

With an elegant smile a wise man mocks the gnawing anxieties of the rich, saying: "The surfeit of the rich will not let him sleep." Although it sometimes happens literally that a rich man, stuffed to indigestion and trying to sleep on a heavy stomach, is kept awake by his own flatulence, still the verse applies rather to the sleep of which the beloved boasts in the Canticle: I sleep but my heart watches. And about which the Psalmist says: "In peace I shall lie down and take my rest."

Note that Solomon does not say someone who *has* wealth but someone who *loves* wealth gains from it no profit. Now there are some elect who, even if they have wealth, do not love it, so do not seek rest in it. But heeding Paul's instruction to the rich not to be haughty or to set their hope on uncertain riches, they give freely, share, and so save up a good capital sum for themselves that they may possess true life and derive no little fruit from their riches. For certainly they will hear from the Lord: "Come, blessed of the Father . . . for I was hungry and you gave me to eat," and so forth.

Now to pass to other failings, about pleasures of the ears, the eyes and other senses, about domination and power, let us consult Solomon, that richest and most powerful but wisest of kings, or rather in him let us listen very attentively to wisdom itself. First, then, speaking for his own person or the person of others, he said: "I said in my heart: I shall go and abound in delights and enjoy good things." And again: "I built palaces, I planted vines, I made gardens and orchards and planted in them trees of every kind." After, much in this vein, he added: "I owned slaves and handmaids and had a very great household. I amassed for myself silver and gold, the treasures of kings and provinces." When he remarked on pleasure of the ears: "I acquired for myself men and women singers," after a few words he added: "Whatever my eyes desired I did not deny them; I did not prevent my heart from enjoying every pleasure, and my heart delighted in what I had prepared."

I ask, what is more comfortable, more attractive, more enjoyable in this life? Yet listen, because nothing is more vain: When I turned to reflect upon all my works and labors, at which I had conceitedly labored, said Solomon, in everything I saw vanity and affliction of spirit, for nothing under the sun endures. So he advanced this general statement, saying: "I have seen everything done under the sun and look! It is all vanity and affliction of spirit."

(*Mirror of Charity* 1:65-66, 68, 77)

True Glory: Charity

What is more pleasant, what more glorious, than through contempt of the world to perceive oneself loftier than the world, and by standing firmly on the peak of a good conscience to have the whole world at one's feet! To see nothing to crave, no one to fear, no one to envy, nothing which another could inflict on oneself! And while one focuses the gaze of the mind on that incorruptible, undefiled and unfading inheritance stored in heaven, how consoling it is with some nobility of mind to despise worldly wealth as perishable, carnal enticements as defiled, worldly pomp as prone to fade away and to exult in the words of the prophet: "All flesh is grass and all its glory like the flower of the field. The grass withers and the flower has fallen but the Lord's word lasts forever." What then is sweeter or what more tranquil, I ask, than not to be agitated by the turbulent impulses of the flesh, not to be seared by the fires of provocations of the flesh, not to be stirred by any seductive sight, but to possess a body cooled by the dew of modesty and subject to the spirit, one which is no longer a seducer to pleasures of the flesh, but a very obedient aide to spiritual exercises? Finally, what is so close to divine tranquility as not reacting to proffered insults, not being terrified by torture or persecution, keeping the same steadfastness of mind in prosperity and adversity, regarding with equal eye both friend and foe, conforming oneself to the likeness of God who makes the sun shine on both the good and the wicked and the rain fall on the just and the unjust?

All these exist together in charity and all exist together only in charity. Likewise in charity true tranquillity and true gentleness exist, because charity is the Lord's yoke. If we bear this at the Lord's invitation we shall find rest for our souls, because the Lord's yoke is easy and the Lord's burden light. In brief, charity is patient and kind, it is not jealous or conceited or boastful, is not ambitious, and so on. For us, then, other virtues are like a carriage for someone weary, food for the traveler's journey, a lamp for those groping in darkness and weapons for those waging battle. But charity, which permits other virtues to be virtues, must exist in all the virtues. It is most particularly rest for the weary, an inn for the traveler, full light at journey's end and the perfect crown for the victor. For what is faith but a carriage to carry us to our fatherland? What is hope but food for the journey to support us in the miseries of this life? What are the four virtues—temperance, prudence, fortitude and justice—but the weapons with which we wage battle? But when death will be fully swallowed up in charity, which will reach its perfection only in the vision of God, then there will be no faith for those for whom the journey here is only begun in faith. Because there is no need to believe in one who is seen and loved. Nor will hope exist, because for someone who embraces God with the arms of charity there remains nothing for which to hope.

Temperance fights against lusts, prudence against errors, fortitude against adversities, and justice against inequities. Yet in charity chastity is perfect and so there is no lust for temperance to fight. In charity knowledge is perfect and so there is no error for prudence to fight. In charity there is true happiness and so no adversity exists for fortitude to conquer. In charity everything is at peace, and so there is no inequity against which justice must remain vigilant. Faith is not a virtue if it does not act through love, nor hope a virtue if what is hoped for is not loved. If you look into this more closely, what is temperance but love that no sensual pleasure entices? What is prudence but love that no error seduces? What is fortitude but love bravely enduring adversity? What is justice but love righting with due moderation the iniquities of this life. Charity, then, begins in faith, is exercised in the other virtues, and is perfected in itself.

This is charity, the consummation of all virtues, the agreeable refreshment of holy souls, the virtuous harmony of our conduct. This is the root from which all good works spring so that they may be good and in which all good works are perfected. The seventh day on which divine grace refreshes us, the month in which, after the deluge of temptations, the arc of the heart gently comes to rest. Temperance protects it, prudence keeps watch over it, fortitude fights for it and justice is its servant.

When the most atrocious beasts of the passions have been removed from our land, that is, from the flesh we bear, God will make us sleep in heavenly slumber. Absorbed in the immense sea of divine brightness, ineffably exalted above ourselves, we shall enjoy perfect freedom and shall see that the Lord himself is God. Celebrating that eternal Sabbath of charity which the holy prophet Isaiah describes: from month to month and from Sabbath to Sabbath, that is, from the Sabbath on which—tasting some beginnings of charity, as far as the day's evil allows—we are given holiday from daily toil, we shall be introduced to that perfect Sabbath when, without disturbing annoyance or disabling misery of the flesh, we will love our Lord God with our whole soul, our whole virtue and all our strength, and our neighbors as ourselves.

(*Mirror of Charity* 1:87-89, 92, 95)

The Enemy of Charity: Self-Centeredness

To take Paul's words as our starting point, we say that the root of all evils is self-centeredness just as, on the other hand, the root of all virtues is charity. As long as this poisonous root remains in the depths of the soul, even though some of the twigs on the surface may be pruned back, others will inevitably continue to sprout from the re-invigorated base until the very root from which these pernicious shoots spring up has been utterly torn out and nothing more remains.

We who seem to have bowed the shoulders of our minds beneath the Gospel yoke, which the Savior's declaration shows to be very easy, and beneath the Lord's burden, which the same authority likewise recommends as very light, we still undeniably toil. Let us who profess the cross of Christ, having taken up the key of God's word, unlock the gates of our breast and, penetrating as far as the division of soul and spirit, of joints and marrow, let us discern the thoughts and intentions of our heart. Without any wheedling flattery, let us scrutinize what lies deeply hidden in the inner recesses of our souls and try harder to tear out the diseased roots themselves.

Of course, this is a toil, not of the flesh but of the heart, just as it is also evident that the rest about which we speak is of the heart and not of the flesh, although outward toil is determined by the quality of a person's inward toil. It should not be said that there is outward toil if there is not already some within. For example: look at hunters and fowlers or whoever else follows such pursuits. If you look closely at their outward physical movements, what is more laborious? If you look at the state of their minds, what is more delightful?

The mind which the Lord's very easy and tranquil yoke—I mean charity—holds in sway will transfer everything that happens to it into its state of tranquillity. It will not permit itself to be upset by any disturbing events but force the very changes of events to contribute to the benefit of its progress. But if a mind is habituated to the very heavy yoke of self-centeredness, its lax restfulness disguises itself as the sweetness of the Lord's yoke as long as there is no occasion for agitation. But as soon as some cause for indignation arises, the savage beast soon bursts from the recesses of the heart as if from a deeply hidden cavern. By the dreadful gnawing of the passions it tears and bloodies the poor soul, allowing it no time for peace or rest. So let this yoke rot in the presence of oil, that is to say, the yoke of self-centeredness in the presence of charity. Then, all of a sudden, someone will experience how light, how easy, how joyful Christ's burden is; how, as someone has said, it catches one up to heaven and snatches one away from the earth.

If we want to experience the sweetness of this rest, let us carefully seek out the causes and roots of our toil, not only pruning with a blunt knife our outward lukewarm attachments but penetrating with vehement desire the very sources of our ills.

(Mirror of Charity 2:3-4)

The Stages of Spiritual Growth

In the first state the soul is awakened, in the second it is purified, and in the third it enjoys the tranquillity of the Sabbath. In the first state mercy is at work, in the second, loving-kindness and in the third, justice. For mercy seeks what is lost, loving-kindness reforms what is found, and justice rewards what is already perfect. Mercy raises up one who is prostrate, loving-kindness aids one who combats, and justice crowns the victor.

What could be a greater indication of divine mercifulness than for that sweetness, that joyfulness, that wonderful serenity in which no defilement intrudes, to impart the grace of its visitation to a soul that has, till then, been defiled? Not only does it shake the soul with terror but, by its force of penetration cutting through all the doors of the mind that have been locked with the bolts of vice, it imprints some kiss of its sweetness on lips still unclean, and by its ineffable amenity coaxes the straying back, draws the hesitant close, and gives new life to the hopeless.

O sweet Lord! What return can I make to you for everything you have given me? Oh, how pleasant your Spirit is in all things! Truly, Lord, your mercy toward me is great. You have stretched your hand down from above, snatching and delivering me from deep waters. . . . You have snatched my soul out of the depths of hell, where I felt a drop of your sweetness on my tongue and heard your voice as if from far off:

> What are you doing, worthless, squalid wretch? Why are you wallowing in squalor? Why are you delighting in shameful deeds? Look at what sweetness there is with me, what pleasantness, what joyfulness! Do you despair because of the enormity of your sins? But shall I, who pursue you when you flee from me, reject you when you come to me? Shall I, who embrace and draw you to myself when you turn your face from me, push you away when you hide under the wings of my mercy?

Your voice, O Lord, your inspiration. From where does such hope for the despairing soul come, if not from your giving, O Lord, you who heal our infirmities in wonderful ways and restore form to our deformity?

But now, what should be said about the second state, in which divine loving-kindness works so wonderfully in us that we profit from temptation and gain greater strength from infirmity? And although every soul naturally flees from toils, temptations and sorrows, we are quickened by so many consolations in the midst of temptations that not only can we endure them when they besiege us but to some extent we can even summon them forth and ask for them when they are slow to appear.

To this state that holy one had progressed who said, "Try me, O Lord, and test me." And further on, "Try me, O Lord, and know my heart."

In this state the mind, accustomed to the countless incentives of heavenly attachments, is moved along little by little to that most sublime kind of visitation experienced by very few.

There it begins to have some foretaste of the first-fruits of its future reward. Passing onto the place of the wonderful tabernacle, right up to the house of God, with our soul melting within us, we are inebriated with the nectar of heavenly secrets. Contemplating with the purest regard the place of our future rest, we exclaim with the prophet: "This is my place of rest forever and ever. Here will I dwell for I have chosen it."

I think it should be noted that although in the first visitation the sweetness of amenity is sometimes mixed with fear, and in the second the goad of fear is often brought to bear along with amenity, still the first has more particularly to do with fear and the second with the sweetness of consolation. But in the third, perfect charity casts out fear. The beginning of wisdom is the fear of the Lord, but the culmination of wisdom is the love of God. The beginning is in fear, the perfection in love. Here is toil, there reward. The first leads up to the second, yet no one attains it except through love itself. Upon the mind often afflicted with fear, beset with grief, cast down by despair, absorbed in sadness and gnawed by listlessness, falls a drop of this marvelous sweetness trickling down from the balsam trees of that rich and densely-forested mountain, as if it were overflowing in a very peaceful downward course. At the splendor of its radiant divine light the whole dark cloud of irrational sensations is dispensed. At its very pleasant taste all bitterness is routed, the heart is expanded, the mind enriched and its capacity for rising upward is primed in a marvelous way. Lukewarmness is banished by fear, and fear is tempered by the taste of divine sweetness. Lest the mind remain sluggish at the lowest levels, fear awakens it. Lest it faint away at toil, affection nourishes it.

Led forth by the alternation of these two until, entirely absorbed by ineffable charity, we burn for the eagerly-desired embraces of him who is the fairest of all the sons of men. We begin to want to depart and to be with Christ, saying each day with the prophet: "Alas for me that my sojourn is prolonged." And so the Lawgiver shall give a blessing, dispensing the wine of compunction along with fear of the Lord to those who are beginning, and milk from the breasts of God's consolation to those who are progressing. And when we are weaned from this milk, we shall feast as soon as we enter his glory.

The first visitation, then, casts reproach on wickedness. The second supports our infirmity. And the third manifests holiness. Let no one boast about the first, therefore, in which the wicked or tepid person is accused, nor about the second in which the weak are tested. And in the third, let anyone who boasts boast in the Lord.

(*Mirror of Charity* 2:26-30)

We Enjoy God and Neighbor

Now it remains for us to show—as God in whose hands we are may deem to inspire both ourselves and our words—what we ought to choose for our enjoyment. In that way we will recognize what we should love and how we should love it.

Since it is evident that we cannot create our own happiness, we see perfectly well that something that is inferior to and lower than our own nature can drag us down by our loving it, not raise us higher. It will bring us misery rather than true happiness. Hence, beginning to reckon ourselves at our proper value and to estimate the privilege of our human nature, we perceive how worthily, how magnificently and how justly the divine law prescribed: You shall adore the Lord your God and God alone shall you serve. That certainly would not have been said if there were some higher nature to whom human nature owed that unique homage or from which it might expect the rewards of blessedness. God should be chosen by us, therefore, in preference to all else, so that we may enjoy the Divine. This is the ground of love. God should be desired above all else; that is the way to progress in love. In attaining to God there will be perfect blessedness because there will be perfect love of the perfect good.

Rightly does the divine law connect the first and greatest commandment with love of God, when it states: "You shall love the Lord your God." Yes, because when we attain this beatifying Good, each of us will enjoy it according to our own capacity. All together, we will be capable of enjoying God to a greater extent than each one of us could singly. So our blessedness will surely be more abundant if, having less capacity for it in ourselves, we begin to possess in another what we cannot have in ourselves. The good of another will not be ours, however, unless we love that good in the other person. And so divine authority very fittingly decreed the second precept: You shall love your neighbor.

Yet, since God will be our highest good, we are commanded to love God always, above all else, in Godself, in us, in others. Therefore, you shall love the Lord your God with your whole heart, all your soul and all your strength. But because our neighbor's good will confers as much joy on us as does our own, we are rightly told: You shall love your neighbor as yourself. It is clear, therefore, that we should choose for our joy these two: God and neighbor, although not in the same way. We should choose God that we may enjoy God in Godself and because of Godself, and our neighbors that we may enjoy them in God and God in them. For although this word "enjoy" is usually taken in a stricter sense—that it may be said that we should take our joy in no other but God alone—still, when speaking to a fellow human, Paul said, "So brother, may I take my joy in you in the Lord."

When we perceive, as we said, that these two should be chosen, and when by contemplation of them everything else has been scorned and we make a choice by consenting, then there really is a foundation for pure love of God and neighbor, because there is a conversion of love itself toward what it should love.

(*Mirror of Charity* 3:25-28)

Those Whom We Can Enjoy in This Life

Charity consists in this: that we choose what we ought for our enjoyment, are moved as we should be and use what we have chosen appropriately. . . . If the choice is healthy and the motion sound, will the use be bad? In tending toward the person loved, intention can be altered and judgment can be deceived. Then, too, with a right intention and an appropriate motion, we may procure the presence of the one whom we have chosen for our enjoyment. Yet in the enjoyment itself we can change our intention, alter the motion and exceed measure. Since we have already given rank to our neighbors on different levels and by diverse merits, we must surely state whether we ought, or whether we can manage, to enjoy all of them or only some of them.

There is a temporal enjoyment by which we can enjoy one another in this life, as Paul enjoyed Philemon. And there is an eternal enjoyment by which we shall enjoy one another in heaven, as the angels enjoy one another, in pure unity of mind. Moreover, since to enjoy means to use something with gladness and delight, I think it evident that at present we by no means can enjoy everyone but only a few persons. It seems to me that we can use some people for testing, some for instruction, some for consolation and some for sustenance. We use our enemies for testing, our teachers for instruction, our elders for consolation and those supplying our needs for our sustenance. Only those whom we cherish with fond attachment, no matter which of these categories they may be in, do we use to sweeten our life and delight our spirit. These persons we can enjoy even at present, that is, we can use them with joy and delight. Charity can be shown to everyone by everyone in this life as far as the choice and interaction are concerned, but as far as enjoyment is concerned, it can be shown to everyone only by a few or even by no one at all. There are few people, if there are any at all, who cherish every sort of human being not only with a rational but even with an attached love.

Finally, charity in both choice and action is shown toward God by many persons to whom the enjoyment of love is not granted in this life but is reserved for the ever-blessed vision of God after this life. There are some, too, who in the light of contemplation and the sweetness of compunction experience a beginning of this sweet enjoyment. But if we are looking toward future joys, these persons should not be said to enjoy God but rather to use God. God grants the ever-pleasant taste of divine sweetness to a good number of people more as a support for their weakness than as a fruit of their love.

Moreover, it is a wondrous consolation in this life to have someone with whom we can be united by an intimate attachment and the embrace of very holy love. To have someone in whom our spirit may rest, to whom we can pour out our soul, to whose gracious conversation we may flee for refuge amid sadness as to consoling songs or to the most generous bosom of whose friendship we may approach in safety amid the many troubles of this world. To whose most loving breast we may without hesitation confide all our inmost thoughts, as to ourselves. By whose spiritual kisses as by medicinal ointments we may sweat out of ourselves the weariness of agitating cares. Someone who will weep with us in anxiety, rejoice with us in prosperity, seek with us in doubts. Someone we can let into the secret chamber of our mind by the bonds of love, so that even when absent in body that one is present in spirit. There, we alone may converse, we two alone, all the more sweetly because more secretly. Alone, we may speak we two alone and once the noise of the world is hushed, in the sleep of peace, we alone may repose we two alone in the embrace of charity, the kiss of unity, with the sweetness of the Holy Spirit flowing between us. Still more, we may be so united we two and approach each other so closely and so mingle our spirits that the two become one.

In this present life we are able to enjoy those whom we love not only by reason but also by affection. Among them, we especially take enjoyment in those who are linked to us more intimately and more closely by the pleasant bond of spiritual friendship. Lest someone think that this very holy sort of charity should seem reproachable, our Jesus himself, lowering himself to our condition in every way, suffering all things for us and being compassionate toward us, transformed it by manifesting his love. To one person, not to all, did he grant a resting place on his most sacred breast in token of his special love, so that the virginal head might be supported by the flowers of his virginal breast, and the fragrant secrets of the heavenly bridal-chamber might instill the sweet scents of spiritual perfumes on his virginal affection more abundantly because more closely. So it is that even though all the disciples were cherished by the sweetness of supreme charity by the most blessed Master, still it was to this one that he accorded this name as a prerogative of yet more intimate attachment: that he would be called that disciple whom Jesus loved.

(*Mirror of Charity* 3:107-110)

Enjoying in the Lord

Let anyone of us who finds it pleasant to enjoy our friends see to it that we enjoy them in the Lord, not in the world or in pleasure of the flesh but in joyfulness of spirit. But, you ask, what does it mean to enjoy "in the Lord"? About the Lord, the apostle Paul said: "By God he has been made for us wisdom, sanctification and justice." Since the Lord is wisdom, sanctification and justice, to find enjoyment in the Lord is to find enjoyment in wisdom, sanctification and justice. By wisdom worldly vanity is banished, by sanctification the vileness of the flesh is forsworn, and by justice all flattery and fawning are checked. Then it is charity, if it comes, as the apostle says, from a pure heart, a clear conscience and unfeigned faith.

A pure heart accepts wisdom, modesty calms the conscience, and unfeigned faith adorns justice. There are those who take enjoyment in vain and ludicrous things, in worldly pomp and mundane spectacles, in the pursuit of vanity and in reveling in falsehood. They do not enjoy themselves in wisdom nor in him who is the strength of God and the wisdom of God. . . . Since they do not enjoy themselves in the sanctification, which consists of the gentleness of charity, they do not, of course, enjoy the Lord who was made our sanctification by God. There are others who take enjoyment in flattery, patting each other on the back and conniving with each other. While taking care not to offend one another, they incur each other's ruin, because they do not enjoy themselves in the liberty of justice or in the Lord.

If our mutual exchange of words is delightful, let our talk be about our habits and about scripture. Let us now grieve together over the miseries of the world, now rejoice together in the hope of future happiness. Let us now refresh one another by confiding our mutual secrets, now long together for the blessed vision of Jesus and for heavenly well-being.

If we relax our tense spirits with some pleasant and less lofty subjects, as is sometimes useful, let these moments of relaxation be nonetheless virtuous and free of frivolity. Although the subjects may not be weighty, let them not lack constructiveness. Let us enjoy one another in sanctification, so that we may know how to possess our vessel—that is to say, our own body—in sanctification and honor and not in passionate desires. Let us take enjoyment in justice, so we may mutually encourage one another in the spirit of freedom. Let us correct one another, knowing that corrections from a friend are better than an enemy's deceitful kisses.

Most beloved Father, these are my meditations on charity. If its excellence, its fruits and the appropriate way of showing it are by them made like an image to appear, this book may be called a *Mirror of Charity*, as you have directed. Yet I beg you not to display this mirror in public for fear that, instead of charity gleaming from it, the likeness of its author may make it dingy.

If, to my great embarrassment, as I fear, you do publish it, by that sweet name of Jesus I entreat the reader not to think

The Sabbaths of Love

As Jesus openly declared, he did not come to abolish the Law and Traditions of the Covenant of his People. Rather he came to fulfill them, bringing them together on a higher plan in his one new commandment: Love as I have loved. In the same spirit, Aelred takes the Hebrew Law and Traditions of the Sabbaths of Rest and calls us to the Sabbaths of Love.

Three Sabbaths—Three Loves

We read in the Old Testament about certain distinctions of Sabbaths. As a matter of fact, in the Law you have three times consecrated to the Sabbath rest: the seventh day, the seventh year and after seven times seven years, the fiftieth year. The first, then, is a Sabbath of days, the second of years and the third is, not inappropriately, called the Sabbath of Sabbaths. It consists of seven Sabbaths of years plus one, so that the number seven, which proceeds from unity and is perfected in unity, may be concluded in unity. In like manner, every good work is founded on faith in the one sole God and progresses by the seven-fold gift of the Holy Spirit to reach the One who is truly one, where all that we are is made one with God. And because there is no division in unity, let not the mind run in various directions. Let it be one in the One, with the One, through the One, around the One, sensing the One, savoring the One—and because always one, always resting, and therefore observing a perpetual Sabbath.

Let us listen to the Lord! "You shall love the Lord your God with all your heart, with all your soul and with all your mind, and you shall love your neighbor as yourself. On these two commandments depend all the Law and the Prophets." If, therefore, we believe—or better, because we believe—the truth, we must look for the distinctions between these Sabbaths in these two commandments, for they come from the Law. Yet if you diligently examine these two commandments, you discover that three things must be loved: yourself, your neighbor and God. When it says, You shall love your neighbor as yourself, it is clear that you ought also to love yourself. This is not a commandment, because it is inherent in our nature. None of us has ever hated our own flesh, so the apostle testifies. If we do not hate our flesh, much less do we hate our mind. Every one of us, even if unwittingly, loves our mind more than our flesh. There is not one of us who would not choose physical infirmity over mental unsoundness.

Let love of self, then, be our first Sabbath, love of neighbor the second, and love of God the Sabbath of Sabbaths. The spiritual Sabbath is rest for the spirit, peace of heart and tranquillity of mind. This Sabbath is sometimes experienced in love of oneself. It is sometimes derived from the sweetness of brotherly or sisterly love. And, beyond all doubt, it is brought to perfection in the love of God. Surely we should be careful to love ourselves in a suitable way, love our neighbor as ourselves, and love God more than ourselves, and not love either ourselves or our neighbor except for God's sake.

Although there is an evident distinction in our triple love, a marvelous bond nevertheless does exist among the three, so that each is found in all and all in each. None of them can be possessed without all. And when one wavers they all diminish. If we do not love our neighbor or God, we do not love ourselves, and if we do not love our neighbor as ourselves we do not love ourselves. Furthermore, someone of us who does not love our neighbor is proven not to love God. For how can we who do not love the brother or sister we see love God whom we do not see?

In some way, then, love of neighbor precedes love of God. Likewise, love of self precedes love of neighbor. It precedes it, I say, in sequence, not in excellence. It precedes that perfect love about which was said: You shall love the Lord your God with all your heart, with all your soul and with all your mind. Of course, a certain part of this love, even if not its fullness, necessarily precedes both love of self and of neighbor. Without it both of these are dead and, consequently, non-existent. It seems to me that love of God is, so to speak, the soul of the other loves. It lives of itself with perfect fullness, its presence communicates to the others their vital being, its absence brings about their death.

That we may love ourselves, the love of God is formed in us; that we may love our neighbor, the capacity of our heart is enlarged. Then as this divine fire grows warmer little by little it wondrously absorbs the other loves into its fullness, like so many sparks. And so it leads all the soul's love with it to that supreme and ineffable good where neither self nor neighbor is loved for self or for neighbor but only insofar as each fades away from self and is borne totally into God.

Meanwhile, these three loves are engendered by one another, nourished by one another, and fanned into flame by one another. Then they are all brought to perfection together.

What is more, it happens in a wondrous and ineffable way that although all three of these loves are possessed at the same time—for it cannot be otherwise—still all three are not always sensed equally. At one moment that rest and joy are sensed in the purity of one's own conscience. At another time, they are derived from the sweetness of brotherly love. At another they are more fully attained in the contemplation of God. Just as some king who possesses various perfume cellars enters now this one, now that, and is steeped in the fragrant scent now of this kind of perfume, now of that, so we preserve within the enclosure of our consciousness several cellars filled with spiritual treasures. As we enter now this one, now that, we balance the measure of our joy with the variety of our treasures.

(*Mirror of Charity* 3:1-5)

The Seventh Day—True Self Love

When we withdraw from exterior commotion into the secret retreat of our mind and, once the gate is closed on the throng of noisy trifles around us, we survey our inner treasures, we find nothing disturbed, nothing disordered, nothing to torment or worry us but rather everything pleasant, everything harmonious, everything peaceful, everything tranquil. The entire throng of our thoughts, words and deeds, like a very well-ordered and very peaceful family, will beam on our spirit like a father's household. This gives rise to marvelous security and from security comes a marvelous joy. And joy gives rise to a kind of jubilation, which bursts out yet more devoutly in God's praise the more clearly we recognize that whatever good there is in us is God's gift.

This is the joyful solemnity of the seventh day. Six days must precede it, that is, the perfection of deeds. First we sweat at good works and then, at last, we pause in tranquillity of conscience. For purity of conscience, by which love of self is judged, is born of good works. Just as we who act evilly or love iniquity do not love our own soul but hate it, so also we who love and accomplish works of justice do not hate but love our soul.

This is the joyful solemnity of that first Sabbath. On it no servile works-of-the-world are performed in even the slightest way; on it the shameful fire of concupiscence is not lighted and the burdens of the passions are not carried.

(Mirror of Charity 3:6)

The Seventh Year—Love of Neighbor

Yet if from the quite secret chamber in which we celebrate this first Sabbath we direct ourselves to that inn within where we rejoice with those who rejoice, weep with those who weep, are weak with those who are weak, burn with those who are scandalized, and sense there that our soul is united with the souls of all our sisters and brothers by the cement of charity and are not vexed by any pricks of envy, set afire by any heat of indignation, wounded by darts of suspicion or consumed by the gnawing of rapacious sadness, then we clasp all of them drawing them into the deep peace that is ours. There we embrace and cherish them all with tender affection and make them one heart and one soul with ourselves. At the delightful taste of this sweetness the whole tumult of self-centered desires soon falls silent and the din of evil habits quiets down. Within there is a complete holiday from everything harmful and in the sweetness of neighborly love an agreeable and joyful interlude.

The apostle Paul, who kept continual Sabbath, is a witness that in the quiet of this Sabbath neighborly charity permits no evil habits to dwell. For he said this: You shall not commit adultery, you shall not steal, you shall not bear false witness, and if there are any other commandments, they are summed up in this sentence: You shall love your neighbor as yourself.

Steeped in the rest and pleasantness of this Sabbath, the prophet David burst into a song of festive thanksgiving: "Behold, how good and pleasant it is when brothers and sisters dwell together in unity." Truly good, truly pleasing. Good surely, because nothing is more useful; pleasing because nothing is more sweet. Just as only one day is set aside for the first Sabbath—it is evident that it is one because it consists of the tranquillity of one's own conscience—so it is not without reason that an entire year is devoted to this Sabbath. Just as a year is made up of many days, so also in the fire of charity one heart and one soul are molten from many souls.

(Mirror of Charity 3:7-8)

The Preceding Six Years

If you wish to carve some mystical significance out of those six years which precede this spiritual Sabbath, know that there are six kinds of persons on whom the spirit's love must be exercised. Just as a year is made up of many days, so also in each of these kinds there are many people united to us by the bond of love.

Our love turns first of all in the order of nature to our blood relatives. Since to have this love is inherent in our very nature, not to have it is extremely inhuman. . . . If we love our own as we ought we already approach this spiritual Sabbath a little. This love, since it proceeds from nature itself, is sanctioned in first place among the precepts having to do with love of neighbor: "Honor your father and your mother."

From here our love goes out to those who are linked to us by a bond of special friendship or who are bound to us by an exchange of services. It expands from a heart in some way grown larger. Still, this love does not go beyond the justice of the Pharisees to whom was said, "You shall love your friend and hate your enemy." Surely love practiced in either of these earns slight reward, for natural law impels us to do this and grace urges us on.

That our love may grow larger, therefore, let it also embrace those who are subject to the same yoke of profession as we. This love will certainly not be cheated of its reward, because it is given for God's sake. In this we cling to Jesus' garments and taste some of that ointment which, running down from the head of the true Aaron, flowed into our beard and reached even the hem of our garment. Anointed by its richness, the heart yet expands. Into its widened love it first receives all those whom that ointment, by its touch, makes partakers of the name of Jesus. Anointed by the Anointed, that is to say, by Christ, they are called Christians.

There still remain two other classes of persons. If they are held close in love surely nothing will prevent us from enjoying the rest of that true Sabbath. We grieve over the ignorance of those who are still outside. . . . We must have compassion . . . and with a devoted attachment pray for them so that they, too, may be found with us in our Lord Jesus Christ.

From there we should pass onto that love in which consists the summit of fraternal charity. In it, we are made sons and daughters of God; in it the likeness of divine goodness is more fully restored in us. As our Savior said in the gospel: Love your enemies and do good to those who hate you. Pray for those who persecute and slander you that you may be sons and daughters of your God who is in heaven.

After that, what will remain but the seventh year, during which we are not allowed to ask our debtors for payment, during which the slave is granted freedom? Those of us who know how to look even our enemies straight in the eye are the ones who can really say, Forgive us as we forgive. Everyone who commits sin is a slave of sin. We are delivered up to this deplorable servitude until, ourselves loving and forgiving, we are forgiven and loved. From being a slave, we then become not only a free person but even a friend.

This is truly a time of peace, a time of quiet, a time of tranquillity, a time of glory and exultation. What trouble, what disturbance, what grief, what anxiety can tarnish the joy of those of us who, from that first Sabbath on which we feed upon the fruits of our labors, progress by a fuller grace to this divine likeness? There, embracing the whole human race in the one love, we are not troubled by any injury from anyone. Rather, just as a very fond parent has a tender affection for a dearly-beloved child suffering delirium, so likewise will we not think unkindly of our enemies, so that the more injured we are by them, the deeper will be the attachment of charity by which we have compassion on those inflicting trouble on us.

(*Mirror of Charity* 3:8-12)

The Sabbath of Sabbaths—
the Love of God

The greater our devotion, the more securely do we, purified by this twin love, pass to the blissful embraces of the Lord's divinity. Thus inflamed with intense desire, we go beyond the veil of the flesh and, entering into that sanctuary where Christ Jesus is spirit before our face, we are thoroughly absorbed by that ineffable light and unaccustomed sweetness. All that is bodily, all that is sensible, and all that is mutable are reduced to silence. We fix our clear-sighted gaze on what is and is so always and is in itself, on the One. At leisure it sees that the Lord is God, and in the tender embrace of charity itself it keeps a Sabbath, doubtlessly the Sabbath of Sabbaths.

This is the jubilee year in which we return to our possession, that is, to our Creator, so that God may truly be possessed by us and possess us, be held by us and hold us, be taken by us and take us. This is the possession that was sold for the price of cheap sin when our love slipped away from the One who made us and clung to the thing that had been made. Not without reason is the number fifty applied to this Sabbath on which servile fear is cast out, concupiscence of the flesh is not only silenced but the memory of it is lulled to sleep and the fullness of the spirit is received. The Spirit is indeed given on the first Sabbath and on the second too! But on the Sabbath of Sabbaths the Spirit's fullness is poured out.

The number seven is kept in each case but it is in the multiplication of seven that the development of this charity is recognized. For the seventh day is, as it were, the foundation of charity, the seventh year its increase and the fiftieth year—which comes after seven times seven—its fullness. On each of these there is rest, on each of these there is leisure, on each of these there is a spiritual Sabbath. First there is rest in purity of conscience, then in the very pleasant joining together of many minds and finally in the contemplation of God.

On the first Sabbath we keep free from fault, on the second from self-centeredness and on the third from absolutely everything that dissipates us. On the first Sabbath we taste how sweet Jesus is in our humanity; on the second we see how perfect he is in charity, and on the third how sublime in his Godhead. On the first we are recollected within ourselves, on the second we are extended outside ourselves. On the third we are caught up above ourselves.

(*Mirror of Charity* 3:17)

The Way of Friendship

By his own confession friendship was something important to this very sociable man from his earliest years. When Aelred entered Rievaulx he brought in with him (as every monk does, from Bernard of Clairvaux to Thomas Merton) who he is and his life's experiences. This is evident in Aelred's writing which touch upon the history and nobility of his times, the saints of its shrines and his sister's vocation as well as what deeply touched his own personal life. Aelred's youthful study of the *De amicitia* (On Friendship) of Marcus Tullius Cicero, an important part of every classical education, many years later remains the humanist fabric into which Aelred weaves the fullness of the gospel's call to friendship as taught and exemplified by Christ and lived in its fullness in the most blessed Trinity.

The teaching of this dialogue is important as the elaboration and fulfillment of Aelred's basic treatise, *The Mirror of Charity*, where already he began to set forth his theological and pastoral understanding of this way of Christian holiness. While friendship among men, which would blossom in an almost mythological chivalry, is one of the great literary themes of the Middle Ages, finding its basis in sacred scripture as well as classical texts, Aelred's contribution is significant because it is so really personal and so profoundly God-centered without losing any of its rich humanism. Unlike his great Christian master, Augustine of Hippo, for Aelred, speaking from his own life's experience, the flow from physical love filled with sentiment and emotion to something more platonic and on ultimately to divine love was a continuous flow without gaps. For Aelred it is an ideal worth striving for, worth the high price it costs, for it is the way to true holiness and complete fulfillment.

Reverting to one of his favorite literary forms, Aelred couches his teaching in conversations or dialogues with some of his young monks, notably here a monk named Ivo.

The Nature of Friendship

Ivo: In the first place, I think we should discuss the nature of friendship. So as not to appear to be painting in emptiness, as we would, indeed, if we were unaware of the precise identity of that about which an ordered discussion on our part should proceed.

Aelred: But surely you are satisfied, as a starting point, with what Tullius [Cicero] says, are you not? "Friendship is mutual harmony in affairs human and divine coupled with benevolence and charity."

Ivo: If that definition satisfies you, I agree that it satisfies me.

Aelred: In that case, those who have the same opinion, the same will, in matters human and divine, along with mutual benevolence and charity, have, we shall admit, reached the perfection of friendship.

Ivo: Why not? But still, I do not see what the pagan Cicero meant by the words "charity" and "benevolence."

Aelred: Perhaps for him the word "charity" expresses an affection of the heart and the word "benevolence," carrying it out in deed. For mutual harmony itself in matters human and divine ought to be dear to the hearts of both, that is, attractive and precious, and the carrying out of these works in actual practice ought to be both benevolent and pleasant. . . . You can, however, get some idea of the nature of friendship from the definition, even though it should seem somewhat imperfect.

Ivo: Please, will I annoy you if I say that this definition does not satisfy me unless you unravel for me the meaning of the word itself?

Aelred: I should be glad to comply with your wishes if only you will pardon my lack of knowledge and not force me to teach what I do not know. Now I think the word *amicus* [friend] comes from the word *amor* [love], and *amicitia* [friendship] from *amicus*. For love is a certain "affection" of the rational soul whereby it seeks and eagerly strives after some object to possess it and enjoy it. Having attained its object through love it enjoys it with a certain interior sweetness, embraces it and preserves it. . . .

A friend is called a guardian of love or as some would have it, a guardian of the spirit itself. Since it is fitting that my friend be a guardian of our mutual love or the guardian of my own spirit so as to preserve all its secrets in faithful silence, let him, as far as he can, cure and endure such defects as he may observe in it; let him rejoice with his friend in his joys and weep with him in his sorrows and feel as his own all that his friend experiences.

Friendship, therefore, is that virtue by which spirits are bound by ties of love and sweetness and out of many are made one.

(*Spiritual Friendship* 1:10-21)

Friendship is Eternal

Aelred: Even the philosophers of this world have ranked friendship not with things casual or transitory but with the virtues which are eternal. Solomon in the *Book* of *Proverbs* appears to agree with them when he says: "He that is a friend loves at all times," manifestly declaring that friendship is eternal if it is true friendship. If it should ever cease to be, then it was not true friendship, even though it seemed to be so.

Ivo: Why is it, then, that we read about bitter enmities arising between the most devoted friends?

Aelred: God-willing, we shall discuss that matter more amply in its own place. Meantime remember this: He was never a friend who could offend him whom he at one time received into his friendship; on the other hand, that other has not tasted the delights of true friendship who even when offended has ceased to love him whom he once cherished. For "he that is a friend loves at all times." Although he be accused unjustly, though he be injured, though he be cast in the flames, though he be crucified, he that is a friend loves at all times. Our Jerome speaks similarly: "A friendship which can cease to be was never true friendship."

(*Spiritual Friendship* 1:21-24)

A Virtue Worth Striving For

Ivo: Since such perfection is expected of true friendship . . . it seems to me that I am exerting myself uselessly in striving after this virtue which I, terrified by its admirable sublimity, now almost despair of ever acquiring.

Aelred: "Effort in great things," as someone [Julius Pomerius] has said, "is itself great." Hence it is the mark of a virtuous mind to reflect continually upon sublime and noble thoughts, that it may either attain the desired object or understand more clearly and gain knowledge of what ought to be desired. Thus, too, we must be supposed to have advanced not a little who have learned, by a knowledge of virtue, how far we are from virtue itself. Indeed, the Christian ought not to despair of acquiring any virtue, since daily the divine voice from the gospel reechoes. "Ask, and you shall receive."

(*Spiritual Friendship* 1:25-27)

The Difference Between Charity and Friendship

Ivo: Are we then to believe that there is no difference between charity and friendship?

Aelred: On the contrary, there is a vast difference; for divine authority approves that more are to be received into the bosom of charity than into the embrace of friendship. For we are compelled by the law of charity to receive in the embrace of love not only our friends but also our enemies. But only those do we call friends to whom we can fearlessly entrust our heart and all its secrets; those, too, who, in turn, are bound to us by the same law of faith and security.

(Spiritual Friendship 1:31-32; 58-59)

Three Kinds of Friendship

Aelred: Let one kind of friendship be called carnal, another worldly and another spiritual. The carnal springs from mutual harmony in vice; the worldly is enkindled by the hope of gain; and the spiritual is cemented by similarity of life, morals and pursuits among the just. The real beginning of carnal friendship proceeds from an affection which like a harlot directs its step after every passer-by, following its own lustful ears and eyes in every direction.

Worldly friendship, which is born of a desire for temporal advantage or possessions, is always full of deceit and intrigue; it contains nothing certain, nothing constant, nothing secure; for, to be sure, it ever changes with fortune and follows the purse. Hence it is written: "He is a fair-weather friend and he will not abide in the day of your trouble." Take away his hope of profit and immediately he will cease to be a friend. This type of friendship the following lines very aptly deride:

A friend, not of the man, but of his purse is he,
Held fast by fortune fair, by evil made to flee.

Spiritual friendship, which we call true, should be desired, not for consideration of any worldly advantage or for any extrinsic cause but from the dignity of its own nature and the feelings of the human heart so that its fruition and reward is nothing other than itself. Whence the Lord in the gospel says: "I have appointed you that you should go and should bring forth fruit," that is, that you should love one another. For true friendship advances by perfecting itself, and the fruit is derived from feeling the sweetness of that perfection. And so spiritual friendship among the just is born of a similarity of life, morals and pursuits, that is, it is "a mutual conformity in matters human and divine united with benevolence and charity."

(Spiritual Friendship 1:38-46)

A Stage Toward the Love
and Knowledge of God

Aelred: Matters of such importance still remain to be said on the good of friendship that, if some wise person were to carry them through to the end, you would think we had so far said nothing. Nevertheless, turn your attention briefly to the manner in which friendship is, so to say, a stage toward the love and knowledge of God. Indeed, in friendship there is nothing dishonorable, nothing deceptive, nothing feigned, whatever there is, is holy, voluntary, and true. . . . In friendship are joined honor and charm, truth and joy, sweetness and good-will, affection and action. And all these take their beginning from Christ, advance through Christ, and are perfected in Christ. Therefore, not too steep or unnatural does the ascent appear from Christ, as the inspiration of the love by which we love our friend, to Christ giving himself to us as our Friend for us to love. Thus charm follows upon charm, sweetness upon sweetness and affection upon affection. Friend cleaving to friend in the spirit of Christ is made with Christ one heart and one soul. Mounting aloft through degrees of love to friendship, we are made one spirit with Christ in one kiss. Aspiring to this kiss the saintly one cries out: "Let him kiss me with the kiss of his mouth."

(Spiritual Friendship 2:18-21)

God is Friendship

Ivo: What does this all add up to? Shall I say of friendship what John, the friend of Jesus, says of charity: "God is friendship"?

Aelred: That would be unusual, to be sure, nor does it have the sanction of the scriptures. But still what is true of charity, I surely do not hesitate to grant to friendship, since the one who abides in friendship, abides in God, and God in that person.

In Praise of Friendship

Aelred: I do not presume that I can explain friendship in a manner befitting the dignity of so signal a good, since in human affairs nothing more sacred is striven for, nothing more useful is sought after, nothing more difficult is discovered, nothing more sweet experienced and nothing more profitable possessed. For friendship bears fruit in this life and in the next.

It manifests all the virtues by its own charms. It assails vices by its own virtue. It tempers adversity and moderates prosperity. As a result, scarcely any happiness whatever can exist among humankind without friendship. A man is to be compared to a beast if he has no one to rejoice with him in adversity, no one to whom to unburden his mind if any annoyance crosses his path or with whom to share some unusually sublime or illuminating inspiration. "Woe to him that is alone, for when he falls, he has none to lift him up." He is entirely alone who is without a friend.

But what happiness, what security, what joy to have someone to whom you dare to speak on terms of equality as to another self, one to whom you need have no fear to confess your failings, one to whom you can unblushingly make known what progress you have made in the spiritual life, one to whom you can entrust all the secrets of your heart and before whom you can place all your plans. What, therefore, is more pleasant than so to unite to oneself the spirit of another and of two to form one, that no boasting is thereafter to be feared, no suspicion to be dreaded, no correction of one by the other to cause pain, no praise on the part of one to bring a charge of adulation from the other. "A friend," says the Wise Man, "is the medicine of life." Excellent, indeed, is that saying. For medicine is not more powerful or more efficacious for our wounds in all our temporal needs than the possession of a friend who meets every misfortune joyfully. So, as the apostle says, shoulder to shoulder, they bear one another's burdens. Even more—each one carries his own injuries even more lightly than that of his friend. Friendship, therefore, heightens the joys of prosperity and mitigates the sorrows of adversity by dividing and sharing them. Hence, the best medicine in life is a friend. Even the philosophers took pleasure in the thought. Not even water, nor the sun, nor fire do we use in more instances than a friend. In every action, in every pursuit, in certainty, in doubt, in every event and fortune of whatever sort, in private and in public, in every deliberation, at home and abroad, everywhere friendship is found to be appreciated, a friend a necessity, a friend's service a thing of utility. "Wherefore, friends," says Julius, "though absent are present, though poor are rich, though weak are strong, and—what seems stranger still—though dead are alive." And so it is that the rich prize friendship as their glory, the exiles as their native land, the poor as their wealth, the sick as their medicine, the dead as their life, the healthy as their charm, the weak as their strength and the strong as their prize. So great are the distinction, memory, praise and affection that accompany friends that their lives are adjudged worthy of praise and their death rated as precious. And, a thing even more excellent than all these considerations, friendship is a stage bordering upon that perfection which consists in the love and knowledge of God. From being a friend of our fellows we become the friends of God, according to the words of the Savior in the gospel: "I will not now call you servants but my friends."

(*Spiritual Friendship* 2:9-14)

The Consummation of Friendship

Aelred: This is that extraordinary and great happiness which we await. God himself actively engenders between himself and his creatures whom he has elevated . . . so much friendship and charity that each one of us loves another as we do ourselves. And by this means, each one of us as we rejoice in our own so do we rejoice in the good fortune of another. Thus the happiness of each one individually is the happiness of all, and the total happiness of all is the possession of each individual. There one finds no hiding of thoughts, no dissembling of affection. This is the true and eternal friendship that begins in this life and is perfected in the next. Here it belongs to the few where few are good, but there it belongs to all where all are good. Here probation is necessary since there is a mingling of wise and unwise; there they need no probation, since an angelic and, in a certain manner, divine perfection beatifies them. To this pattern then let us compare our friends, whom we are to love as we do ourselves, whose confidences are to be laid bare to us to whom our confidences are likewise to be disclosed, who are to be firm and stable and constant in all things. Do you think there is any human being who does not wish to be so loved?

The day before yesterday, as I was walking the round of the cloister of the monastery, the brethren were sitting around forming as it were a most loving crown. In the midst, as it were, of the delights of paradise with the leaves, flowers and fruits of each single tree, I marveled. In that multitude of brethren I found no one whom I did not love and no one by whom, I felt sure, I was not loved. I was filled with such joy that it surpassed all the delights of this world. I felt, indeed, my spirit transfused into all and the affection of all to have passed into me, so that I could say with the prophet: "Behold, how good and how pleasant it is for brethren to dwell together in unity. . . ."

How delightful friends find it to converse with one another, mutually to reveal their interests, to examine all things together and to agree on all of them! Added to this there is prayer for one another, which, coming from a friend, is the more efficacious in proportion as it is more lovingly sent to God, with tears which either fear excites or affection awakens or sorrow evokes. And thus a friend praying to Christ on behalf of his friend, and for his friend's sake desiring to be heard by Christ, directs his attention with love and longing to Christ. Then it sometimes happens that quickly and imperceptibly the one love passes over into the other and coming, as it were, into close contact with the sweetness of Christ himself, the friend begins to taste his sweetness and to experience his charm. Thus ascending from that holy love with which he embraces a friend to that with which he embraces Christ, he will joyfully partake in abundance of the spiritual fruit of friendship, awaiting the fullness of all things in the life to come. Then, with the dispelling of all the anxiety which now causes us to fear and be solicitous for one another, with the removal of all the adversities which now we must bear for one another and, above all, with the destruction of the sting of death together with death itself, whose pangs now often trouble us and force us to grieve for one another, with salvation secured, we shall rejoice in the eternal possession of

Supreme Goodness. And this friendship, to which here we admit but few, will be outpoured upon all, and by all outpoured upon God, and God shall be all in all.

(*Spiritual Friendship* 3:79, 82, 133)

Aelred's Experience

I recall now two friends, who, although they have passed from this present life, nevertheless live to me and always will so live. The first of these I gained as my friend when I was still young, in the beginning of my conversion, because of a certain resemblance between us in character and similarity of interests. The other I chose when he was still a boy and after I had tested him repeatedly in various ways, when at length age was silvering my hair, I admitted him into my most intimate friendship. Indeed, I chose the former as my companion, as the one who shared in the delights of the cloister and the spiritual joys which I was just beginning to taste, when I, too, was not as yet burdened with any pastoral duty or concerned with temporal affairs. I demanded nothing and I bestowed nothing but affection and the loving judgment of affection according as charity dictated. The latter I claimed when he was still young to be a sharer in my anxieties and a co-worker in these labors of mine. Looking back, as far as my memory permits, upon each of these friendships, I see that the first rested for the most part on affection and the second on reason, although affection was not lacking in the latter nor reason in the former. In the end, my first friend, taken from me in the very beginnings of our friendship, I was able to choose, as I have said, but not to test. The other, devoted to me from boyhood even to middle age and loved by me, mounted with me through all the stages of friendship, as far as human imperfection permitted. And indeed, it was my admiration for his virtues that first directed my affection toward him. It was I who long ago brought him from the South to this northern solitude and first introduced him to regular discipline. From that time he learned to conquer his own flesh and to endure labor and hunger. To very many he was an example, to many a source of admiration and to myself a source of honor and delight. Already at that time I thought that he should be nurtured in the beginnings of friendship, seeing that he was a burden to no one but pleasing to all. He came and went, hastening at the command of his superiors, humble, gentle, reserved, sparing of speech, a stranger to indignation and unacquainted with murmuring, rancor and detraction. He walked as one deaf, hearing not and as one dumb not opening his mouth. "He became as a beast of burden," submissive to the reins of obedience, bearing untiringly the yoke of regular discipline in mind and body. Once when he was still young he was in the infirmary, and he was rebuked by my holy father and predecessor for yielding so early in life to rest and inactivity. The boy was so ashamed at this that he immediately left the infirmary and subjected himself with such zeal to corporal labor that for many years he would not allow himself any relaxation from his accustomed rigor, even when he was afflicted with serious illness. All this in a most wondrous way had bound him to me by the most intimate bonds and had so brought him into my affection that from an inferior I made him my companion, from a companion a friend, from a friend my most cherished of friends. When I saw that he had advanced far in the life of virtue and grace, I consulted the brethren and imposed upon him the burden of the subprior's office. This went against his will, to be sure, but because he had vowed himself to obedience, he modestly accepted. Yet he pleaded with me in secret to be relieved of it, alleging as excuse his age, his lack of knowledge and finally the friendship which we had but lately formed. He feared that this might prove to be an occasion for him either to love the less or to be loved the less. But, availing nothing by these entreaties, then he began to reveal quite freely but at the same time humbly and modestly what he feared for each of us and what in me pleased him but little. He hoped thereby, as he afterwards confessed, that I would be offended by this presumption and would the more easily be inclined to grant his request. But his freedom of speech and spirit only led our friendship to its culmination, for my desire for his friendship was lessened not a whit. Perceiving then that his words had pleased me and that I answered humbly to each accusation and had satisfied him in all these matters, and that he himself had not only caused no offense but rather had bene-fitted more, he began to manifest his love for me even more ardently than before, to relax the reins of his affection and to reveal himself wholly to me. In this way we tested one another, I making proof of his freedom of utterance and he of my patience. And I, too, repaid my friend in kind in his turn. At an opportune moment, thinking that I should harshly reprove him, I did not spare him any reproaches, and I found him patient with my frankness and grateful. Then I began to reveal to him the secrets of my innermost thoughts and I found him faithful. In this way love increased between us, affection glowed warmer and charity was strengthened until we attained that point where we had but one mind and one soul to will and to not will alike. Our love was devoid of fear and knew no offense. It shunned suspicion and abhorred flattery. There was no pretense between us, no simulation, no dishonorable words, no unbecoming harshness, no evasion, no conceal-ment. Everything was open and above board, for I deemed my heart his and his mine. And he felt in like manner toward me. And so we progressed in friendship without any deviation. Neither's correction evoked the indignation of the other, neither's yielding produced blame. So, proving himself a friend in every respect, he provided as much as was in his power for my peace and my rest. He exposed himself to dangers, and he forestalled scandals in their very inception. Occasionally I wanted to provide for his ailments with some creature comforts. He opposed it, saying that we should be on our guard against having our love measured according to the consolations of the flesh, and of having the gift ascribed to my carnal affection rather than to his need with the resultant effect that my authority might be diminished. He was as it were my hand, my eye, the staff of my old age. He was the refuge of my spirit, the sweet solace of my grief. His loving royal wrath. Only Jonathan, who alone could be somewhat justifiably envious, thought it proper to oppose his father, to defer to his friend and to offer him counsel in the face of opposition. Preferring friendship to a kingdom, "You," he said, "shall be king, and I will be next after you." And see how Saul, the father of the youth, strove to arouse envy in him against his friend, heaping him with reproaches, terrifying him with threats, reminding Jonathan that he would be despoiled of a kingdom and deprived of honor. But when Saul had uttered the sentence of death against David, Jonathan did not fail his friend. "Why shall David die? Wherein has he sinned? What has he done? He put his life in his hands and slew the Philistine and you rejoiced. Why, therefore, shall he die?" At this utterance the king became so angered he strove to nail Jonathan to the wall with his spear. Adding reproaches to threats, he said. "You son of a woman that is the ravisher of a man, I know that you love him to your own confusion and to the confusion of your shameless mother!" Then he spewed out poison to steep the heart of the youth, the word that was an inducement to ambition, a ferment of envy, an incentive to emulousness and bitterness: "As long as the son of Jesse lives, your kingdom will not be established." Who would not be stirred by these words, who would not be made envious? Whose love, whose favors, whose friendship would these words not corrupt, diminish or obliterate? That most loving youth, preserving the laws of friendship, brave in the face of threats, patient before reproaches, despising a kingdom because of his friendship, unmindful of glory but mindful of grace, declared. "You shall be king, and I will be next after you. . . ." Behold, Jonathan was found a victor over nature, a despiser of glory and of power, one who preferred the honor of his friend to his own, saying: "You shall be king, and I will be next after you." This is true, perfect, constant and eternal friendship that envy does not corrupt nor suspicions diminish nor ambition dissolve. Tempted, it does not yield; assailed, it does not fall. It is unyielding though struck by reproaches innumerable and though wounded by injuries manifold. Therefore, "go and do you in like manner."

(*Spiritual Friendship* 3:92-96)

Aelred's Beloved Ivo

Indeed, the fond memory of my beloved Ivo, yes, his constant love and affection are, in fact, always so fresh to my mind, that though he has gone from this life in body, yet to my spirit he seems never to have died at all. For there he is ever with me. There his devout countenance inspires me. There his charming eyes smile upon me. There his happy words have such relish for me that either I seem to have gone to a better land with him or he seems still to be dwelling with me here upon earth.

(*Spiritual Friendship* 2:5)

Aelred's Eulogy for His Dear Simon

Grief prevents me from going further. The recent death of my dear Simon forcibly drives me instead to weep for him. Perhaps this was the cause of that fear which disturbed my mind at night. Perhaps this was the cause of the nightmares which robbed me of needed rest; that is, that my most beloved friend was to be suddenly snatched from this earth. It is no wonder my mind had so disturbing a premonition of his death, since it took joy with such delight in his life. See how the fear that I feared has now overtaken me, how what I dreaded has come to pass. Why do I pretend? Why am I silent? Very likely because that tribulation still hovers above me. Let what is concealed in my heart spring to my eyes and to my tongue. If only, if only, yes, if only the heart of a mourner might exude in teardrops and rivulets of words that sorrow born in its inner depths. Have pity on me, have pity on me, if any of you are my friends, for the hand of the Lord has touched me. You are astonished that I am weeping. You are still more astonished that I go on living! For who would not be astonished that Aelred goes on living without Simon, except someone who does not know how sweet it was to live together, how sweet it would be to return together to the fatherland. So bear patiently with my tears, my sighs, the moaning of my heart, then.

And you, my beloved, you have been brought into the joy of the Lord. You feast with delight at the table of the great father of our family and in the kingdom of the Father with your Jesus you are happily inebriated on that new fruit of the vine. Still permit me to offer you my tears, to disclose my attachment to you and, if possible, to pour out my whole spirit for you. Do not forbid these tears which your memory evokes, my beloved brother. Let not my sighing burden you, for it is prompted not by despair but by attachment. Do not restrain my tears, which flow not from lack of faith but from tenderness. If you remember where you have arrived, what you have escaped, where you have left your close friend, you will assuredly realize how justified is my grief, how worthy of tears my wound. Let me alone, then, that I may assuage my sorrow. Mine, I say, mine, for your death is not to be wept over when it was preceded by a life so praiseworthy, so lovable, so pleasing to all, a life commended by your amazing conversion, your remarkable way of life and your blessed perseverance.

Really, your conversion was amazing! Who would not be amazed, who would not marvel that a frail young boy, distinguished by birth, remarkably handsome, should have taken to such a life and in such a way. You took your leave, my gentle brother, knowingly unknowing and wisely unwise. Like the first patriarch, abandoning your fatherland, your kin, and your father's home, you went by a route unknown to you, you arrived at a place you did not know. But he who was leading you knew, he who had already enkindled your young heart with the flame of his love to run in the scent of his perfumes. Fairest of all the sons of men, he went before you, anointed with the oil of joy above his fellows, anointed with the spirit of wisdom and understanding, the spirit of counsel and forti- tude, with the spirit of knowledge and piety. And you continued to run to the scent of his perfumes. That spiritual heart preceded you over rough and mountainous places, scat- tering on his path the aromas of myrrh, frankincense, and all the perfume of merchants' powders, and you continued to run to the scent of his perfumes. The boy Jesus preceded this boy, showing him the manger of his poverty, the resting place of his humility, the chamber of his charity decked with the blossoms of his grace, rich with the honey of his sweetness, strewn with the balsam of his consolation. And you continued to run to the scent of his perfumes. I do not know what great, what ineffable foretaste your mind had even then, that it believed a diet of hay should be fed to its frail body fainting from hunger as if to a wearied beast of burden. The devout boy fled from the face of his father, but even more, to the face of his Father. He wanted to forget his own people and his father's home, that a King, the King's Son, might desire his beauty and they might be two in one spirit, as far as he who was his Son's Father by nature might become his son's Father by grace.

O wonderful devotion! O wonderful self-forgetfulness! It was not enough for him to rival the venerable patriarch Joseph who, leaving to the Egyptian woman the cloak by which he was held fast, slipped naked from the clutches of his captor. In addition this zealous pursuer of evangelical perfection took no thought for the morrow. With no provisions, he undertook a wearisome enough route. As his limbs grew more and more faint from fasting, he said, "I heard that servants of Christ feed on grass. Why don't we, too?" Turning aside a bit from the path, he began to pluck some grass and said: "Oh, how delicious!"

O good lad, how did it taste to you? What is that grass, I ask, but faith, that hay but charity? He tasted Jesus in his heart, of course, and so the hay in his mouth. Whence, I ask, whence did these come to the lad? They are yours, Lord Jesus. You give and accept, provide and exact. Who gives you anything not your own? But if anyone wished to give you something that he had not accepted from you, you would not deign to accept it. Therefore, Lord Jesus, that boy accepted; he accepted from you and made return, he accepted and offered. He accepted and offered this devotion of his mind, this fervor of faith, this ardor of love.

All things belong to you, Lord. You consecrated the beginnings of his conversion by these marvels, you received afterwards the pleasing sacrifice of his devout life and you have now mercifully transferred that most acceptable holocaust to your temple on high. There my Simon, my gentlest friend but your poor one, Lord Jesus, rests in the bosom of Abraham. There he rests transferred from death to life, from labor to rest, from misery to blessedness.

See how I, who began to grieve, have found reason to rejoice. Clearly I have found reason, but in you, my beloved brother, not in myself. Do not weep for me, he said, but for yourselves and for your children. For you, beloved brother, for you I rejoice but for myself I feel keen sorrow. For you one should rejoice, yet I should be wept over because I must live without Simon. What a marvel that I be said to be alive when such a great part of my life, so sweet a solace for my pilgrimage, so unique an alleviation for my misery, has been taken away from me. It is as if my body had been eviscerated and my hapless soul rent to pieces. And am I said to be alive? O wretched life, O grievous life, a life without Simon! The patriarch Jacob wept for his son, Joseph wept for his father, holy David wept for his dearest Jonathan. Simon, alone, was all these to me: a son in age, a father in holiness, a friend in charity. Weep, then, poor fellow, for your dearest father, weep for your most loving son, weep for your gentlest friend. Let waterfalls burst from your creased brow, let your eyes shed tears day and night. Weep, I say, not because he was taken up but because you were left.

Who will allow me to die with you, my father, my brother, my son? I would not wish to die instead of you. This would be to consider not your interests but my own. Holy David kept repeating this about his son, the parricide: Absalom, my son, my son Absalom, who will allow me to die instead of you? David did not say that about his friend Jonathan, did he? Nor Joseph about his father? It had to be said about the parricide, it had to be said about the sinner, because the death of sinners is worst of all. It was pious to wish to die for an impious man that he might live to repent, live to weep, live to receive God's mercy so that he might not perish forever. But those who departed in peace were not afterwards to be recalled to this misery nor to be subjected again to so many fears, so many sorrows.

Then again, Rachel weeping for her children refused to be consoled. Why was she weeping? Attachment. But her attachment would be consoled, if her son were recalled from death, if the mother again enjoyed the sight of him. But Rachel did not wish this. Why? Because if the son were recalled from death, he would be cast precipitately from blessedness into misery. She wished not that her son be recalled to life, but that she be taken up to her son in eternal rest. Attachment demanded sons but reason resisted attachment so that the sons might not be recalled. Divine providence delayed taking her up. Therefore, Rachel weeping for her children refused to he consoled.

My case is the same, I grieve for my most dear one, for the one-in-heart with me who has been snatched from me, and I rejoice that he is taken up to eternal tabernacles. My attachment seeks his sweet presence that nourished it delightfully, but my reason does not agree that this soul, beloved by me, once free from the flesh should again be subject to the miseries of the flesh. My soul along with his, a part of its own, longs to enjoy the embrace of Christ but my weakness resists, my iniquity resists, and even divine providence resists this. Surely, the one who was ready entered the marriage feast with the Bridegroom, but to me, wretch that I am, the door is still closed. If only, Lord Jesus, if only that door be opened one day. But I hope in your mercy, Lord, that someday it will be opened. I have sent my first fruits on ahead, sent on my treasure, sent on no small part of myself. Let the rest of me follow on after you. Where my treasure is, there let my heart be also.

Here now, O Lord, I shall follow his ways that in you I may enjoy his company. I was able to do so, Lord, though at a slow pace, when my eyes observed his devout way of life, when the sight of his humility blunted my pride, when the thought of his tranquillity calmed my restlessness, and when the bridle of his admirable seriousness checked my levity. I remember that often when my eyes were darting here and there, at one glimpse of him I was filled with such shame that, suddenly recovering myself, I checked all that levity by the strength of his seriousness and, pulling myself together, I began to employ myself in something useful. The authority of our Order forbade conversation; his appearance spoke to me, his walk spoke to me, his very silence spoke to me. His appearance was modest, his walk mature, his speaking serious, and his silence without bitterness.

Finally, during this last year of his life, as if he were not unaware of what he was called to, with what tranquillity, what peace, what circumspection he completed his life! Oblivious to everything external, even to me, and enclosed within the confines of his own mind, he seemed to have portrayed quite exactly the one whom the holy prophet Jeremiah describes: "It is good for a person when such a person has borne the yoke from youth. Such a one will sit alone and be silent because that one has exalted self above self." Indeed, he shouldered the yoke of discipline in the flower of youth, Lord Jesus, choosing that narrow way which leads to life. He chose "in the sweat of his brow to eat his bread" and to submit his will to another's judgment. What is more, even from his youth he bore the heavy yoke of poor health, with which for eight years, even to the last, I believe, with fatherly attachment you scourged him without remission. Therefore, finding almost nothing outside in which to delight, he withdrew to the interior solitude of his mind, sitting alone and being silent but not listless in his inactivity. He used to write or read or devote himself privately to meditation on the scriptures for which his senses were always keenly alert. He hardly ever spoke of necessities, even with the prior. He walked about like a deaf man, not hearing, like a dumb man not opening his mouth, become like one not hearing and having no rebuke on his lips. Indeed if anyone, seizing the occasion, approached him, such gentleness soon marked his speech, such cheerfulness without any dissipation appeared on his face, that his moderation in speaking and his humility in listening disclosed how free of bitterness and how full of sweetness was his silence.

Look at what I have lost. Look at what I miss. Where have you gone, O model for my life, harmonizer of my conduct? Where have you gone, where have you vanished? What shall I do? Where shall I turn? Whom now shall I propose to follow? How have you been torn from my embrace, withdrawn from my kisses, removed from before my eyes? I embraced you, dear brother, not in the flesh but in the heart. I used to kiss you not with a touch of the lips but with affection of the mind. I loved you because you welcomed me into friendship from the very beginning of my conversion, showed yourself more familiar with me than with the others, linked me with your own Hugh in the inner depths of your soul. So great was your love for both of us, so similar your affection, so single your devotedness that, as I gathered from your words to me, your attachment preferred neither one to the other, though unbiased reason would have preferred him to me because of his holiness. Why then did you pass away while I was not there? Why did you not want me present at your departure, whom alone when I was present you thought took the place of both? Perhaps you thought we should be spared this, that is, you and I, so that your departure would not cause affliction to my sight, and my grief would not sadden your joyful and tranquil departure even in the slightest way. Or perhaps, as I am inclined to believe, the divine loving-kindness came upon you in your aloneness in order to transfer your calm and peaceful soul in all tranquillity. God would take you from the miseries of this life

to your longed-for fatherland. Almost without your knowing
it, divine Love would break the bond of your physical dwelling
with such gentleness that not the slightest fear of death might
trouble a soul so divinely cherished.

The one who was resting near your bed detected in you no
sign of impending death. Rather, your cheerful mien and
greater facility in speaking increased his hope of your recovery.
When, gently reclining your head, you gave up your spirit, he
believed that you had fallen asleep, not that you had passed
away. For you, my beloved brother, for you it was meant to be
that way, that you passed away with such tranquillity. By your
very peaceful death you showed quite clearly that you were
welcomed by ministers of peace. No wonder. You did not
dread but rather desire that hour, for on the day before you left
us, you said to the superior of our monastery when he visited
you that you hoped not to tarry longer in this life.

What then did you gain, bitter death? What did you gain?
Of course, you invaded his tent, the site of his pilgrimage, you
broke the chain that tethered him. You did destroy the
dwelling he enjoyed for a time, but you removed the load
which oppressed him. "We know that if the earthly house we
inhabit is destroyed," said the apostle, "we have a building
from God not made with hands, an eternal home in heaven."
Now, therefore, his soul, friend of virtues, desirous of quiet-
ness, eager for wisdom, victorious over nature, has been
divested of its enveloping flesh. And, if I may say so, he has
flown off on freer wings to that pure and sublime Good to be
gathered into the long desired embrace of Christ.

But, you object, the flesh once committed to the earth is
reduced to ashes. Yes, of course. Then why rejoice?

The flesh is dead so that it may be brought to life, dissolved
so that it may be renewed yet better. Sown in weakness, it will
rise in strength. Sown in corruption, it will rise in incorrup-
tion. Sown in dishonor, it will rise in glory. Lastly, sown an
animal body, it will rise a spiritual body. O death, where is
your victory? O death, where is your sting? Where you seem to
have done something to him, you are shown to have been

profitable to him. So you spewed all your poison over me. Seeking him, you inflicted dire wounds upon me. Me, what sorrow, what bitterness, what harshness I bore, because I lost my guide on the journey, the mentor for my way of life.

But why, O my soul, did you gaze so long without tears on his dear mortal remains? Why did you bid farewell without kisses to that body so dear to you? I grieved and moaned, poor wretch, and from my inmost being drew long sighs, but yet I did not weep. I realized that I should be grieving so hard that even when I was grieving exceedingly, I did not believe I was grieving at all. So I felt afterwards. My mind was so numb that even when his limbs were at last uncovered for washing, I did not believe he had passed on. I was astonished that he, whom I had clasped to myself with the bonds of sweetest love, suddenly had slipped from my hands. I was astonished that this soul which was one with mine could, without mine, cast off the shackles of his body. But my numbness at last gave way to feelings, gave way to grief, gave way to compassion. Now, O my eyes, what are you doing, what are you doing? I beg you, do not be sparing, do not pretend. Offer whatever you have, whatever you can, over the remains of my beloved. Why do I blush? Am I the only one to weep? Look at how many tears, how many sobs, how many sighs surround me! Are these tears reprehensible? Yet the tears you shed over the death of your friend excuse us, Lord, for they express our affection and give us a glimpse of your charity. You took on the emotion that belongs to our weakness but only when you wished it. You were also able not to weep. Oh, how sweet are your tears and how gentle. What savor and consolation they give to my troubled mind. Look at how he loved him, they said. And look at how my own Simon was loved by everyone, embraced by everyone, cherished by everyone! But perhaps some stalwart persons at this moment are passing judgment on my tears, considering my love too human. Let them think as they please. But you, Lord, look at them, observe them. Others see what happens outside but do not heed what I suffer within. That is where your eyes see, O Lord. Certainly in my eyes your servant had nothing to hinder his passing over into your embrace.

"No one knows what goes on in another human being, except the human spirit which is within him." But your eye, O Lord, cuts through the dividing line of soul and spirit, of joints and marrow and discerns the thoughts and intentions of the heart. As an excellent servant [Augustine] said: "What hope is there for one's life, praiseworthy though it may be, if you judge it without mercy." Look at the source of my fear, O Lord, look at the source of my tears. Heed them, O most tender-loving, dearest and most merciful Lord. Receive them, O my only hope, my one and only refuge, the object of my intentions, my God, my mercy! Receive them, O Lord, as the sacrifice I offer you for my most beloved friend and, if any flaws remained in him, either pardon them or impute them to me. Let me, let me be struck, let me be scourged. I shall pay for everything. I ask only that you do not hide your blessed face from him, do not withdraw your sweetness or delay your kindly consolation. Let him experience the sweetness of your mercy, my Lord. He desired it so ardently, anticipated with such great assurance, commended with such great attachment. He savored it with such delight that night when, after the others had retired to rest and only one brother was left at his bedside, in thanksgiving he cried out aloud, "Mercy! Mercy! Mercy." He was trying, they say, to recite in full the verse of the Psalm: Mercy and justice shall I sing to you, O Lord. Stopped, I think, by the sweetness of that first word, lingering familiarly over it, at last he turned to the one seated by his bed and repeated the word over and over. Then he noticed his attendant was overcome with drowsiness. As if indignant at such lack of responsiveness—the other was obviously not plunged into the same sweetness, enjoying a similar savor—with his hand he began to rouse him from a sleep, repeating in a more clear and powerful voice: "Mercy! Mercy!"

What is it I see in this, my Lord? Surely, as with my own eyes, I seem to discern his mind refreshed by the draught of this verse. He was freed by ineffable joy as he saw his sins absorbed in the immense sea of divine mercy. There was nothing left to burden it, nothing to darken his conscience in the least. What a joy to behold his soul, washed in the fountain of divine mercy after laying down the weight of sin. It reaches upwards with most agile movements, following its natural impulse, exulting to divest itself at any moment of the remnants of the flesh. It meditates on the great mercy of God on whom it relies absolutely. Ah, return now to your rest, O soul, because the Lord has treated you kindly. Pass to the place of the wonderful tabernacle, even to the house of God, with a shout of joy and confidence and the songs of those called to the feast. I shall follow you with my tears, whatever their worth. I shall follow you with my affection. I shall follow you with the unique sacrifice of our Mediator. And you, Father Abraham, again and again extend your hands to receive this poor man of Jesus, another Lazarus. Open your arms, welcome into your bosom, lovingly receive, cherish and console someone returning from the miseries of this life. To me, also, a wretch, albeit his beloved, grant a place of rest some day with him in your bosom. Amen.

(Mirror of Charity 1:98-114)

The Friend

There is no doubt at all that Aelred's spiritual teaching is centered on Christ. Christ appears in every single one of the sermons he preached in the chapter at Rievaulx, and some of them are almost totally devoted to him.

Aelred certainly does not neglect that transcendent community to which Christ belongs and from which he comes forth. His Trinitarian teaching is precise and beautiful. It is to the Trinity "to which the whole of our faith turns." Although the Father, Son and Spirit manifest themselves diversely as Voice, Man and Dove, they are absolutely one. "Whatever we think about God, it must end in unity. . . . If we think of wisdom, virtue, strength, providence, goodness or anything else, all this is one in God. For the Father, Son and Spirit are one," in what they are and in what they do. Jesus shows his greatest love to us when he sends into us the Holy Spirit, "who is the love and unity of the Father and Son, so that by that unity and that charity, by which they are essentially one, we are in a certain sense made one in them and with them, not by an identity of substance but by an adhesion of spirit. . . ."

That we might arrive at transcendent oneness with the divine Trinity, the Son has become one with us. In this we have more reason to rejoice than the angels. For although the Son became incarnate also to remedy the angels' ruin, it is our human nature he assumed. "What a great thing: God and man joined in one person, the fall of the human family is repaired, death is destroyed, life is renewed, the ruin wrought by the angels is restored, and the whole world is reconciled." Aelred delights in wonder at this divine condescension: "eternity making a new start, strength itself weak, bread hungry, the fountain thirsty. . . ." "He who created all, who ruled all, who filled all, who sustained all, bowed beneath the hands of his servant."

There is a vital concreteness in Aelred's appreciation of the incarnation, almost a sensuality. "It is a great pleasure, brothers, to see the Lord on the breast of his mother, to see him in the manger, to see him today in the arms of the blessed Simeon. It is a great pleasure to imagine in our hearts his words, his miracles, his embrace, his kiss." He sees Jesus strip himself to be baptized and John touching him with his hands. Jesus seeks and embraces us with a maternal affection and we are to embrace him. "It is so beautiful to see him, so charming to hear him, so sweet to taste him, so lovable to embrace him. . . ."

In the course of Aelred's sermons almost every aspect of Christ's life is explored in one way or another, but above all our Lord's passion. Even in a Christmas sermon Aelred exhorts his brothers "Remember his passion; see how he is crowned with thorns." His Easter sermon has a detailed meditation on the passion "for so we come to the glory of the resurrection." And Aelred emphasizes that Jesus did it all for us. "He was born for us, he was tempted for us, he was beaten for us, he died for us . . . he rose for us." In it all

Jesus sought to give us an example, to give us hope. Jesus is our whole way and our end. "Blessed is the one who . . . receives our Lord Jesus Christ . . . who willingly thinks of him and delights in him . . . ponders and judges how he can please him, by what works, what words, what thoughts . . . that you might rest in his embraces, so that you can be free and see how sweet he is, experience that he is sweet, sense that his Spirit is sweeter than honey. . . ."

If we gather up all the names that Aelred gives our Lord Christ, we have a magnificent litany. Christ is our Physician, our Spouse, King, Remunerator, the Wisdom of God, Justice, Sanctification and Redemption, the Lamb, the Poor One, Strength, Sweetness, the Power of God, Light, the New Adam, the Eagle that ascended above the heavens, the Author of Creation, the Sun of Justice, the Son of Mary, the Font of all sweetness, King Solomon, the Virgin of virgins, the Lord of the angels, the Font of wisdom, our Peace.

Aelred collects many Biblical images to bring out different facets of Christ: He is cloud and light, a lamb, a bracelet, the ark, the keystone, the sweetest of grapes, bread, the head, the sun—the greater light, the man of the strong woman, wisdom, emperor, a mountain and the mediator. Aelred also calls forth different Biblical personages as types of Christ: Adam, Jacob, Joseph, Elijah, David and Solomon. And he fills this out with collections of statements from the New Testament, such as in his Twenty-Eighth Sermon: "the 'Mediator between God and the people,' 'our Ruler and our Judge,' 'the Lord our lawgiver' who was sent to the wretched to be for us not only 'high priest of good things to come' but also 'King of kings and Lord of lords.'"

At the same time Aelred is capable of setting forth the mystery of Christ with almost scholastic conciseness and clarity:

> In our Lord Jesus there are two natures, the divine and the human. These two natures are so perfect in him that the divine nature was not diminished on account of the human nor the human reduced to nothing on account of the divine. That is why he is at once equal to the Father and less than the Father: equal because of his divinity and less because of his humanity.

Aelred teaches us to build a tabernacle for Christ in our hearts. Christ is to reign in us; Christ is to be a pilgrim in us; Christ is to be identified with us, hungering in us, thirsting in us. We are to be united with Christ in his death. We are to be renewed in his resurrection. And "when Christ our life appears, we will appear with him in glory." All of this is to be accomplished in us through the grace of our Redeemer, Jesus Christ, one with the Father and the Spirit.

It would seem that Aelred could never praise Jesus enough, that he is wholly centered upon him.

The Name of Jesus

His work is in keeping with his name. What name? You know his name. What is the sound, the flavor, the fragrance of his name? It is oil: "Your name is oil poured out." Why oil? Because his name savors of charity, savors of mercy. For what is the meaning of that dear name of Jesus? It speaks of our salvation, for he is my God and my Jesus, that is, my Savior, my well-being and therefore my mercy. He did the work of his wisdom when he created the world. But he had not yet undertaken the work of his mercy. For the work of mercy responds to those who are wretched. He did the work of judgment when he hurled the devil out of heaven for his pride. He did the work of judgment when he expelled a human from paradise for disobedience. In these works he showed his wisdom and power. He wished also to show his mercy, for his mercies are above all his works. Therefore the work of his mercy is said most properly to be his work.

But how should he accomplish this work if not by saving the wretched? Therefore the work of our salvation is the work of his mercy, that is, the work that is most properly his. What is so characteristic of a Savior, that is, Jesus, as to save?

(*Sermon Twelve for Easter*, 16-18)

Saint Paul's Love of the Name

At first there was no name Paul hated so much as the name of Jesus Christ, afterwards nothing seemed so sweet to him as that name. So great was his love for Christ that he was unwilling to bear any longer the name which was his when he was persecuting Christ. It was as if he hated that name because under it he was a persecutor of Christ. Therefore, just as he renounced the zeal of the persecutor, so he wished to rid himself of the name. It was not immediately upon his baptism that he received the name Paul, that is quite clear from the Acts of the Apostles. It was when Christ began to be more fully his delight that his very name and all that he had been previously began to be something he despised. For who can say or even conceive how much Paul loved our Lord? That sweet name, the name of Christ, was always in his heart, always on his lips, so that he could hardly ever utter a word without always adding that name. As you read and hear in his epistles, in almost every verse he always inserts: "In Christ Jesus" or "In Christ Jesus our Lord" or "Through Jesus Christ our Lord." Before, he rejoiced when he could put any of the Lord's disciples in bonds or cast them into prison or stone them, now when he suffers all these things, he glories all the more. And therefore he says: "I find happiness in my infirmities, in insults, in hardships suffered for Christ."

(Sermon Fifteen for the Feast of Saints Peter
and Paul, 20-21)

The Love of Christ

We know that both Peter and Paul loved Christ greatly and were loved greatly by Christ. And therefore let us love and honor both of them, praising the Lord for the life and death of both. Because the life of both feeds us with its teaching, and the death of both affords us an example of patience. What else can I call them but two seraphim? Seraph means fire, and without doubt both burned wonderfully with the love of God. And both amiably set the hearts of others on fire with that love. Nonetheless we can find some differences in their love.

For in the love that Peter had for the Lord we are encouraged to have a certain warmth of affection for Christ's humanity. It was for Christ's humanity that Peter had the fervor and love of which we spoke a little while ago, as we can show from the gospel. Once when the Lord spoke to his disciples about his passion and said that he was to be betrayed and killed, Peter so tenderly loved him and found his bodily presence so sweet that he said: "Be merciful to yourself, Lord; let this not be." Again when the time arrived to arrest him, an excited Peter snatched up a sword, wishing to prevent from happening what the Lord himself wanted to be. This to be sure he did out of the strong feeling of love he had toward Christ's humanity.

In Paul, however, we are encouraged in that love which we should have for knowledge of Christ's divinity. Whence Paul himself says: "And if we have known Christ according to the flesh, we now know him so no longer."

We can be quite sure that both, Peter and Paul, especially having received the Holy Spirit after the Lord's ascension, knew and loved our Lord Jesus Christ perfectly insofar as a human person can. Yet since some people are so weak as to be quite unable to raise themselves to the knowledge of divinity, while others are so strong that they can contemplate even what is divine and heavenly, the weak have the example of Peter for giving themselves to a certain tender love of Christ's humanity, and the strong have in Paul certain levels of contemplation by which they mount to gaze upon the things of heaven.

(Sermon Fifteen for the Feast of Saints Peter
and Paul, 34-37)

Above All

There remains yet one place higher than all the others. Jesus, who has both built and restored the spiritual ark, sits there alone in his beauty, without peer. By his gentleness he keeps all lower creatures in order. May he give savor to all of them, fill all with his fragrance, enlighten all, shed upon all his splendor and bring all that is lower in a straight line to that single place of his love.

He alone in all, he alone above all, both captures our attachment and demands our love. He claims for himself a place in the abode of our heart, not only the most important place but the highest; not only the highest but also the innermost.

(Mirror of Charity 3:106)

Jesus, the Fragrant Field

This field, as it seems to me, is holy scripture, a fertile field indeed, full of every blessing. "Behold," Isaac says, "the smell of my son is as the smell of a plentiful field, which the Lord has blessed." In this field there is the smell of myrrh and incense and every spice of the perfumer. Truly, brothers, there is no virtue, no insight, no wisdom whose smell is not fragrant in this field. And who is full of every blessing, full of every scent of this field, this plentiful field that the Lord has blessed? Consider. In none of the saints can the fullness of every virtue be found. In David the virtue of humility is specially praised; in Job, one detects the smell of patience with a stronger sweetness. Joseph is chaste, Moses is meek, Joshua is strong, Solomon is wise. Yet of none of these can it be said that his smell is like the smell of a plentiful field. In truth the smell of my dearest Lord Jesus is above every perfume, his smell is like the smell of a plentiful field that the Lord has blessed. Whatever wisdom, whatever virtue, whatever grace is found in the sacred page will all be discovered in him, in whom all the fullness of the godhead dwells corporeally, in whom all the treasures of wisdom and knowledge lie hid, to whom God does not give the spirit by measure, of whose fullness we have all received.

(Sermon for the Feast of Saint Benedict)

The Fragrance of Christ

"Your robes are all fragrant with myrrh and aloes and cassia," O Christ, O Anointed. Oh, how fragrant these robes of yours are! His robes are the members of the body he assumed for us: The Word was made flesh. There is myrrh, there is aloes, there is cassia. Oh, how fragrant are the ointments of our Anointed. He, who in himself was immortal life, became mortal for our sake. Hence myrrh. He, who by the presence of his divinity fills all things for our sake, emptied himself taking on the form of a slave. Hence aloes. He, before whom the angels tremble, humbled himself, becoming obedient unto death—death on a cross. Hence cassia. Myrrh, with which it is customary to anoint dead bodies, signifies mortality. Aloes, which is collected in small drops, signifies the emptying-out, which made him for our sake a little less than the angels. Cassia is a humble plant or tree but fragrant, and it signifies his humility; its fragrance has spread throughout the world. Rightly therefore is your name Christ, rightly the Anointed, rightly oil poured out. That is why the maidens have come to love you whom previously they feared. They have caught the scent of this fragrance of your ointments.

Come then, brothers, let us savor these ointments in our heart by assiduous meditation. Let us consider how sweet the myrrh of his mortality should be to us, by it he has set us free from all mortality; how sweet his abasement, it raises us up to the heavens; how sweet his humility, which exalts us. Let us reflect how low Christ stooped for our sake. Look at these wonders: At the approach of death Christ is sad, while Paul rejoices; Christ weeps at the death of his friend Lazarus, while that mother of the Maccabees does not weep at the frightful death of her seven sons; John the Baptist came neither eating nor drinking, Christ came eating and drinking to be called a glutton and a wine-bibber. . . . To me the tears that you shed at the death of your friend are sweeter than the stoic endurance of the philosophers, who would have the wise one left unmoved by any emotion. More pleasant to me certainly is the smell of your food and drink in the midst of sinners and tax-gatherers than the rigid abstinence of the Pharisees. Certainly the fragrance of your ointments surpasses all scents. How I savor it when I see the Lord of all majesty showing himself, as far as bodily exertion and human emotion are concerned, not like the strong but the weak. What a comfort it is to me in my weakness! Truly this weakness of my Lord without doubt brings me strength and stability in my weakness.

For this reason you who are strong in religious observance and prompt to embrace all sorts of austerities are to be warned not to judge rashly those whom you see accommodating their rigor somewhat to the infirmities of the weak. I am entrusted with the care of my brother's body and soul, for I do not love the whole man if I neglect anything belonging to either—for it is very difficult for the mind not to be tempted when the flesh has too much to suffer. If I see him in distress, whether it be on account of the austerity of the food or because of work or the vigils—if, I say, I see that he is tormented in body and tempted in spirit, if I see him in such affliction and, although provided with the goods of this world, I shut up my heart against him, how can it be said that the divine love dwells in me. If I always follow the rigor of the strong and do not on occasion accommodate myself to the infirmities of the weak, I am not running in the fragrance of Christ's ointments but with the harshness of the Pharisees. They vaunted themselves on their rigorous abstinence and condemned the disciples of the Lord, indeed the Lord himself, calling him a glutton and a wine-bibber. What indeed has to be guarded against is that relaxation and self-indulgence be fostered beneath the appearance of accommodation. Saint Gregory's maxim must be observed: observance without rigidity and compassion without relaxation.

Let us run, then, brothers, let us run in the fragrance of these ointments with which Christ is anointed

(Sermon Three for the Nativity of Our Lord, 29-36)

God and Man

You know well, my brothers, that in our Lord Jesus there are two natures, the divine and the human. These two natures are so perfect in him that the divine nature was not diminished on account of the human nor the human reduced to nothing on account of the divine. That is why he is at once equal to the Father and less than the Father: equal because of his divinity and less because of his humanity. Certainly, brothers, it is a great good and a great joy to know our Lord Jesus Christ in his humanity, in this way to love him and to think of him and, as it were, to see in one's heart his birth, his passion, his wounds, his death, and his resurrection. But a much greater joy has the one who can say with the apostle: "Even if we once knew Christ in the flesh, now we no longer know him in this way." It is a great joy to see how our Lord lay in the manger, but it is a much greater joy to see how the Lord reigns in heaven. It is a great joy to see how he nurses at the breast but a much greater joy to see how he gives food to all. It is a great joy to see him in the arms of a maiden but a much greater joy to see how he himself contains all things in heaven and on earth.

(Sermon Twenty for the Assumption of Saint Mary, 4)

The Way

Dearest brothers, if we wish to ascend to that place from which Christ descended, to the Father on high, let us begin our ascent here. Where? From the Son of Mary, that is, from the humanity of Christ. And let us ascend to his divinity. For he is the way. As he says, "I am the way." Apart from this way no one can come to the Father on high. That is why he says, "No one comes to the Father except through me." For no one can begin anything good unless he begins it from Christ. He is the foundation of all that is good. As the apostle says, "No one can lay any other foundation than that which is already laid, that is, Christ Jesus. . . ."

Let us then, brothers, ascend here and now. And let us begin from Christ and let us go to Christ. Let us begin from Christ in that he is man, and let us go to Christ where he is one with the Father on high. . . . If we wish to ascend to him, the first thing to do is to be converted to him. In this way our increase begins. . . .

But here especially we ought to think of that Star of ours that she may shine upon us in this night, in this darkness. We ought to consider the Beam that has issued from this Star, the Beam who in a way has been darkened for our sakes in order to free us from this darkness. Let us set him against all carnal affection and let us regard him as father, mother, brother, friend. Father, because he instructs us; mother, because he comforts us and nourishes us with the milk of his sweetness; brother, because he has taken flesh from our flesh; friend, because he has shed his blood for us.

This is the direct way. . . .

Then we shall see him whose Spirit is sweeter than honey, whose heritage surpasses honey dripping from the comb. With spiritual arms we shall embrace him and kiss him with wondrous sweetness. Then we shall see and feel how good and how sweet it will be in that blessed life to enjoy the sight of our Creator, to share the company of the angels, to be endowed with the immortality of eternity. Then we shall see him who came down from the bosom of the Father into the bosom of a mother, so that we, beginning as we have said, from his humanity which he assumed from his mother, may come to his divinity which he had with the Father.

(*Sermon Twenty-four for the Nativity of Saint Mary*,
8, 16, 18, 31, 47)

And His Mother

Certainly an important dimension of Aelred's life, love, and teaching would be missing if we did not include some of the expressions of his love of the Blessed Virgin Mary and his understanding and appreciation of her role in the plan of salvation. His devotion to the holy Mother begins to reveal itself in his Annunciation sermons and bursts into full flower in his sermon for the Feast of the Assumption: "How perfect was the heart of the Virgin, in whose heart there was an integral faith. Oh, how blessed is this Lady of ours, who was chosen for such a work, predestined to this above all others. Consider how great was her excellence, who was set as queen and lady over all other creatures, how spotless, how pure she in whom the Holy Spirit made for himself a special dwelling place. The Holy Spirit filled Mary with such an abundance that it was not only enough for the Virgin but for the whole world. All the virtues abounded in Mary."

Aelred speaks a number of times of Mary's virginity, affirming that she was a virgin before, in and forever after the birth of her Son. He perhaps so lauds this virtue in Mary because he was one of those who, as he says, persevered in virginity through her example even in the midst of "torments and pains."

As in the case of her Son, Aelred provides us with a veritable litany in honor of the holy Virgin: She is our Advocate, our Hope, our Mediatrix, our Queen, our Lady, our Mother, our Protector, the most holy Virgin, Vision of Peace, the wholly Beautiful One, Lady of ladies, Queen of queens, our Joy, our Glory, our Hope, our Consolation, our Reconciliation, our Refuge, our Guardian, our Auxiliatrix.

As with Jesus, our abbot reaches out in all directions to find Biblical types and images, which can help him to bring forth her beauty and her role. Mary is Rebecca and Rachel. She is Mary, the sister of Moses, and the virgin Abisag, in the bosom of David. She is a sheep and a fleece, a cloud and light. She is a castle, a village and the east gate. She is the lover of the Song of Songs and King Solomon's strong woman, "the woman about whose strength the Lord warned the serpent." She is the seed of Abraham from which arose the Sun of Justice. She is the Star of the Sea.

"And therefore, dearest brothers, if the whole of me was made a tongue, I could not satisfy my desire to speak of . . . the glory and praise of the most blessed Mother of God. For among all the saints of God she is the more excellent, the more blessed and sweet. . . . And therefore, brothers, we ought always to praise and honor her and with all devotion recall her sweetness."

The Humble Beauty

In all look at her wonderful humility. She who was full of God, greater than the world, higher than heaven, more fertile than paradise, the luster of virgins, the glory of women, the praise of men, the joy of angels, she whom the Son of God chose to be his mother, called herself a handmaiden. She whom the angel greeted subjected herself in all obedience to a workman. She who was queen of heaven, mistress of the angels, she who bore God in her womb, humbly greeted her relative because that relative was older than herself. How right it is then that it is said to the blessed Mary: You are beautiful and fair, most chaste in the midst of delights.

(Sermon Nine for the Feast of the Annunciation, 25)

The Perfection of Blessed Mary

With her whole being the most blessed Mary came to the Wisdom that cries out and says: "Come to me, all you who desire me." That is why these words are read especially on her solemnity. She longed for Christ and therefore she passed over to Christ. Her longing for him was perfect, for from infancy itself she turned from the world for love of him, refused to gratify the appetites of the flesh and made nothing of all the glory of the world. Do not be surprised that I have said that she desired Christ from her infancy, when he was not yet born. After all, the apostle says of Moses: "He considered the reproach attaching to Christ greater wealth than the treasurers of Egypt." Moses lived long before the birth of Christ, and yet

with his eyes on Christ's sufferings he chose to undergo
suffering rather than to rule in Egypt. So it was with the most
blessed Mary. Knowing that Christ was to be born she began
to imitate his way of life, although it had not yet been seen on
earth, just as Moses already imitated his passion although that
had not taken place.

No one therefore so perfectly passed over the sea of this
present life as did blessed Mary. She so perfectly came to
Christ in her heart that Christ also came to her and remained
with her even in body. This is the reason of the fact that
Aaron's sister, who is named Mary, went before the sons of
Israel when they passed through the Red Sea and went before
with a tambourine. For without doubt the most blessed Mary,
the true Mary, whom the other Mary foreshadowed, goes
before all who have passed through this sea, that is the present
world. She leads the way in dignity, in holiness and in purity,
and also in mortification of the flesh, that is, with a tambourine. She leads the way in this also, that she was the first to pass
over. For she was the first of the whole human race who
escaped the curse of our first parents. Therefore she merited
hearing from the angel: "Blessed are you among women," that
is to say, while all women are under a curse, you alone among
them merit this marvelous blessing. Therefore, dearest
brothers, let us imitate, insofar as we can, our most blessed
Lady. Let us desire Wisdom, let us come to Wisdom, who cries
out and says: "Come to me, all you who desire me and be filled
with the fruit of my begettings."

(*Sermon Twenty-two for the Nativity of Blessed Mary*, 12-15)

The Young Mother

But what is the meaning of the Evangelist's statement that
"they did not understand what he had said to them"? It does

not, I think, apply to Mary, for from the moment the Holy Spirit came upon her and the power of the Most High overshadowed her she could not be ignorant of any purpose of her Son. But while the rest did not understand what he had said, Mary, knowing and understanding, "kept all these things in her heart and pondered over them." She kept them by the exercise of memory, she pondered them in her meditation, and she compared them with the other things, which she had seen and heard of him. So the most blessed Virgin was even then making merciful provision for us, in order that matters so sweet, so wholesome, so necessary, might not be lost to memory through any neglect and therefore not written down or proclaimed, with the result that his followers would be deprived of such delightful spiritual manna. This most prudent virgin therefore faithfully preserved all these things, modestly remained silent, then when the time came told of them and entrusted them to the holy apostles and disciples to be preached.

Concerning the following words: "Jesus advanced in wisdom, in years and in favor with God and men," much has been said by many persons, each according to his own judgment, and it is not for me to pronounce on their opinions. Some have held that Christ's soul, from the moment it was created and taken up into God, possessed equal wisdom with God. Others, as if fearing to put a creature on a par with the Creator, have said that he advanced in wisdom just as he did in years, and they appeal to the authority of the gospel, which says: "Jesus advanced in wisdom, years and favor." And it is not surprising, they say, if he is said to have been less in wisdom, since, without any possibility of falsehood, he is stated to have been then mortal and liable to suffering and so less in beatitude. Everyone may judge of these opinions as he wills. For me it is enough to know and to believe that from the moment that the Lord Jesus was taken up into personal union with God, he was perfect God and therefore was and is perfect wisdom, perfect justice, perfect beatitude and in addition perfect virtue. I have no doubt that whatever can be said of

God as to his nature could be said of Christ, even when he was in his Mother's womb. That does not mean that we consider him before the resurrection not to have been liable to death and suffering, since we confess that he was man not merely in appearance but truly. He possessed a true human nature in which he could advance in years. But whether he could advance in wisdom is for those to decide who are competent to discuss such matters.

(*Jesus at the Age of Twelve*, 9)

The Interior Castle

The blessed virgin Mary herself, whose glorious assumption we are celebrating today, was doubtless blest because she welcomed the Son of God in the body, but she was more blest because she had welcomed him in spirit. I would be a liar if the Lord himself had not said this.

Yesterday it was read how a certain woman said to our Lord: "Blest is the womb that bore you and the breasts that nursed you." And the Lord said to her: "Rather blessed are those who hear the word of God and keep it." Therefore, brothers, let us prepare a spiritual castle in order that our Lord may come to us. For I dare to say that if the Blessed Mary had not prepared this castle within herself, the Lord Jesus would not have entered her womb nor her spirit nor would this gospel be read on her feast today. Let us then make this castle ready. There are three things with which a castle is provided in order to make it strong: a moat, a wall and a tower. First the moat, then the wall, rising over the moat, and finally the tower, which is stronger and more important than the other two. The wall and the moat protect one another, since if the moat were not in the way it would be possible to devise a way of approaching the wall and undermining it. And if the wall did not rise above the moat some could approach the moat and fill it up. The tower protects the whole because it is higher than all the other parts.

Let us now enter into our soul and see how all this ought to be realized in us spiritually. What is a moat but deep ground? Therefore, let us dig our heart so that it may be very low ground. Let us take away the earth that is inside and throw it up, for that is the way a moat is made. The earth that we must take and throw up is our earthly fragility. Let not this lie hidden within but let it always be before our eyes, so that in our heart there may be a moat, that is low-lying and deep ground. This moat, brothers, is humility. Remember what the vine dresser in the gospel said about the tree that the owner of the vineyard wanted to cut down because on it he found no fruit: "Leave it, Lord, this one year while I dig around it and manure it." He wanted to make a moat there, that is, to teach humility. In this way, then, brothers, let us begin the building of this castle. For unless this moat, that is, true humility, is first established in our heart, we shall only be able to build something that will fall in ruins about our head. How well the blessed Mary had made this moat for herself! Truly she was more mindful of her own fragility than of all her dignity and holiness. She knew well that her fragility came from herself, that her holiness, that she was the Mother of God, that she was Mistress of the angels and the Temple of the Holy Spirit, came only from God's grace. Therefore, what she was of herself she humbly confessed, saying: "Behold the handmaid of the Lord. Be it done unto me according to your word." And again: "He has looked upon the lowliness of his servant."

After the moat we must make the wall. This spiritual wall is chastity, a wall that is strong indeed and preserves the flesh in its integrity and free from defilement. It is the wall that protects the moat of which we have spoken, so that it may not be filled up by the enemy. For if one loses chastity, the whole heart is at once filled with dirt and filth, with the result that humility, that is, one's spiritual moat, ceases to exist in the heart. But just as this moat is protected by the wall, the wall must be protected by the moat. For the one who loses humility will not be able to preserve chastity of the flesh. Thus it comes about that a virginity which is preserved from infancy itself right up to old age is sometimes lost, because when the soul is defiled by pride the flesh too is defiled by wantonness. Saint Mary had this wall in herself more perfectly than any other human person. For she is the holy and untouched virgin. Her virginity, like the most steadfast of walls, could never be penetrated by any projectile or by any other instrument, that is, by any temptation of the devil. She was a virgin before giving birth, a virgin in giving birth, and a virgin after giving birth. If you are already imitating the most blessed Mary and have this moat of humility and the wall of chastity, it is necessary that you build the tower of charity.

A great tower is charity, my brothers. As the tower is accustomed to be higher than every other part of the castle's edifice, charity is above all the other virtues that form part of the soul's spiritual building. That is why the apostle says: "Now I will show you a far more excellent way." He said this of charity, because it is the more excellent way that leads to life. No one who is in this tower has any fear of his enemies, since perfect love casts our fear. Without this tower the spiritual castle which we are describing is weak. For when those who have the stout wall of chastity, strong as it may be, but either despise or pass judgment on their sisters or brothers instead of showing them the charity they ought to show because they do not have a tower, their enemy passes over the wall and kills their souls. Similarly, if they seem humble in their dress, in their food and in their tastes and yet entertain bitter feelings toward their superiors and their brethren, that moat of humility cannot defend them from their enemies. Who can say how perfectly the most blessed Mary had this tower? If Peter loved the one who was his Lord, how much did the Blessed Mary love the one who was her Lord and her Son! How much she loves her neighbor, that is all men and women, is demonstrated by the many miracles and the many visions by which the Lord has deigned to show that she prays in a special way to her Son for the whole human race. Brothers, it would be superfluous for me to try to show even the beginnings of her charity. So great is it, no mind is adequate to conceive it.

(*Sermon Nineteen for the Feast of the Assumption
of Saint Mary*, 4-14)

Contemplation and Action

As long as you are on earth and I and any other, provided that we are Christ's members, he himself is on earth. As long as those who are his members go hungry and thirsty and are tempted, Christ is hungry and thirsty and is tempted. That is why he will say on the day of judgment: "As long as you did it for one of these the least of mine, you did it for me." Accordingly, brothers, in this wretched and toilsome life, Martha must be present in our house, that is to say, our soul must concern itself with corporal activity. For as long as we need to eat and drink we need to labor. As long as we are tempted by carnal delights we need to subdue the flesh with vigils, fasts and manual labor. This is Martha's part. Mary, also, ought to be present in our soul, that is, spiritual activity. For we should not always be intent on bodily pursuits, but sometimes we should be free to see how good and sweet the Lord is, to sit at Jesus' feet and hear his word. By no means should you neglect Mary for the sake of Martha, nor again Martha for the sake of Mary. For if you neglect Martha, who will feed Jesus? If you neglect Mary, what benefit will it be to you that Jesus entered your house since you have not tasted anything of his sweetness?

Know, brothers, that never in this life should these two women be separated. When the time comes when Jesus is no longer poor nor hungry nor thirsty nor able to be tempted, then Mary alone, that is, spiritual activity, will occupy the whole of this house that is our soul. Saint Benedict saw this, or rather the Holy Spirit in Saint Benedict. That is why he did

not say and lay down that we should only be intent on *lectio* as
Mary and pass over work or Martha, but he commended both
to us, allotting certain times to Martha's work and certain
times to that of Mary.

These two activities were perfectly present in the Blessed
Mary, our Lady. Her clothing of our Lord, her feeding of him,
her carrying him and her flight with him into Egypt, all this
belongs to bodily activity. But that she treasured all these
things, holding them in her heart, that she meditated on his
divinity, contemplated his power and savored his sweetness,
all this belongs to Mary. Whence the evangelist beautifully
says: "Mary, sitting at the feet of Jesus, heard his word." As far
as the role of Martha was concerned, the Blessed Mary did not
sit at Jesus' feet. Rather, I would say, the Lord Jesus himself sat
at the feet of his dearest mother. For, as the evangelist says:
"He was subject to them," that is, to Mary and Joseph. But in
as much as she saw and knew his divinity, assuredly she sat at
his feet, for she humbled herself before him and reckoned
herself as his handmaid. In the role of Martha she attended to
him as one weak and small, hungry and thirsty. She grieved
when he suffered and the Jews heaped outrages on him. That is
why she is told: "Martha, Martha, you are troubled and
anxious about many things." In the role of Mary she addressed
supplications to him as the Lord, worshiped him as Lord, and
yearned with all her might for his spiritual sweetness.

Therefore, my brothers, as long as we are in this body, in
this exile, in this place of penance, let us realize that what is
most proper and most natural for us is what the Lord said to
Adam: "You shall gain your bread by the sweat of your brow."
This belongs to Martha. Whatever we taste of spiritual sweetness is only, I might say, a certain pittance with which God
sustains our weakness. Let us then, dearest brothers, carry out
Martha's role with all solicitude and let us exercise ourselves
with all fear and care in the role of Mary and let us not
abandon the one role for the sake of the other. It will sometimes happen that Martha will want to have Mary with her at
her work, but she must not be granted her desire. "Lord, do

you not care that my sister has left me to get on with the work by myself? Tell her to help me." This is a temptation. See therefore, brothers, that when, during the time that we should devote to *lectio* and prayer, the thought occurs to us that we ought to go to such and such a task as if it were necessary, then as it were Martha calls Mary to help her. But the Lord judges well and justly. He does not bid Martha sit down with Mary, neither does he bid Mary to get up and serve with Martha. Mary's role is indeed the better and it is more pleasant and delightful. Yet he does not wish that Martha's task should be left undone on account of it. Martha's role is more laborious, yet he does not wish Mary's repose to be disturbed. What he desires therefore is that both should do their own parts.

Whoever, however, understands this in the sense that there are some who should do nothing in this life but follow Martha's part and others again who should give all their attention to Mary's part assuredly errs and fails in understanding. Both of these women are in the one castle, both in the one house, both are pleasing and acceptable to the Lord, both are loved by the Lord, as the evangelist says: "Now Jesus loved Mary, Martha and Lazarus." Which of the holy Fathers ever came to perfection without both of these activities?

Since, however, each one of us must practice both of these roles, we must clearly do what belongs to Martha at certain times and at other times what belongs to Mary, unless necessity comes upon us, which is not governed by law. Therefore we must be solicitous to keep to those times which the Holy Spirit has determined for us. At the time of *lectio* we must stay still and quiet, not yielding to idleness or drowsiness, not departing from Jesus' feet, but sitting there and hearing his word. But when it is time for work we should be active and prompt and on no account should we omit the ministry of love in order to obtain quiet. We should never switch from the one activity to the other unless obedience—to which we ought never prefer repose or work, action or contempla-tion—compels us to leave, as we might say, the very feet of Jesus. For certainly, although Mary would find greater pleasure in sitting at Jesus' feet, if the Lord told her to do so she would get up and serve with her sister without the least demur. But the Lord did not tell her to do so in order to give his approval thereby to both activities and to make us careful, if no other command is given us, always to preserve both roles and not abandon one for the sake of the other.

We must also consider the Lord's words: "Mary has chosen the best part which shall not be taken away from her." The Lord has given us great consolation in these words. Martha's part will be taken away from us but Mary's part will not be taken away. Who would not grow weary of these labors and miseries if they were to be always with us? That is why the Lord consoles us. Let us then act manfully. Let us manfully endure these labors and miseries, knowing that they will come to an end. Again, who would care much for these spiritual consolations if they did not last longer than this life? But Mary's part will not be taken away from us, rather it will be increased. What here we begin to taste in some tiny drops, after this life we will drink until we enjoy a certain spiritual inebriation. As the prophet says: They will be inebriated with the rich plenty of your house, and you will let them drink from the flowing stream of your delights. Let us not then be vanquished by these labors, for they will be taken away from us. Let us yearn hungrily for a taste of the divine sweetness, for here indeed it begins, but after this life it will reach its perfection in us and remain with us for all eternity. May the blessed Mary plead for us with her Son, our Lord, that we may obtain this happiness. He lives and reigns with the Father and the Holy Spirit, God, through all the ages of ages. Amen.

(Sermon Nineteen for the Feast of the Assumption
of Saint Mary, 20-31)

Mary's Great Love

This virgin purer than all other virgins, holier than all other women, stronger than all men, fairer than the sun, more ardent than fire, our David provided for himself. He knew her, indeed it was he who made her such for himself and yet he chose to seek her out through his servants. Solomon sought for her when he said: Who shall find a valiant woman? Isaiah sought for her and found her. That is why he says: "Behold a virgin shall conceive and give birth to a son, who will be given the name Emmanuel." Jeremiah sought for her and found her. And in his wonder declared: "The Lord has created something new on the earth: A woman shall encompass a man." Finally, holy Gabriel sought her and invited her to the embraces of the true David. She alone it was in whose bosom the true David could rest more intimately. Her embrace would warm him more sweetly. With her he could sleep more quietly in his bed. This is our Lady, Saint Mary, in whose sacred breast the flame of love had not died down. She loved him more than anyone else did, and so she yearned for him more and therefore sought him with greater care. But now her soul loves him whom until now her flesh loved.

That is why she says: "In my bed I sought him whom my soul loves." She does not say whom my soul loved but whom my soul loves. For then so to speak it was her flesh that loved him. Although, the force of divine love wholly possessed her most holy soul so that she could rightly be called a Sunamite—for Sunamite means "scarlet" and that is the color of fire. She was on fire with the flame of love, red with the blaze of divine love. Therefore, although she loved God with her whole soul, nonetheless, because she was still concerned about her own salvation and that of the whole world which he still had to work out by means of his flesh, she longed for his humanity. She still thought of him in the flesh. She sought him in the flesh. And her soul loved him in the flesh.

(*Sermon Twenty for the Feast of the Assumption*, 20-22)

Mother of Sorrows

See, brothers, and, if you can, conceive and picture to your-selves how the blessed Mary felt in regard to her dearest Son today, to what glory she came, how perfectly the love and knowledge of his divinity absorbed her. That is why she says that up to this time she did not find him, even though she gave birth to him from her womb. This we have said of her first seeking. She sought him again through his passion, after his death. This was a quest full of sorrow and anxiety. Then was holy Simeon's prophecy in her regard fulfilled: "And your soul a sword shall pierce." A sword of pain, a sword of grief, a sword of compassion.

What streams of tears then burst from her chaste eyes when she saw her Son, such a Son, hanging on the cross, given gall to drink and mocked by wicked men. With what pain did she hear him say: "Woman, behold your son," telling her to receive a disciple in the place of a Son, a servant in the place of her Lord! Then indeed a sword of sorrow pierced her soul, plunging to the very place where soul and body divide. Then without doubt she sought him whom her soul loves. She sought him with love, sought him with yearning, so that she did not escape the lament of the apostle: "The flesh lusts against the spirit and the spirit against the flesh." As far as her natural affection was concerned I have no doubt that she wished then to set her Son free from that death to silence the Jews' mocking or even, if possible, to undergo the death herself. Then, too, it was night, for so much distress over-clouded all her joy, so much grief almost deprived her of reason. Therefore she sought him then but did not find him, because that natural desire of hers that her Son should not suffer was not granted so that through her Son's death her eternal salvation might be fully accomplished.

(*Sermon Twenty for the Feast of the Assumption*, 27-29)

The Assumption of Blessed Mary

Today, Saint Mary entered that heavenly court, saw the white robes of the virgins, the ruddy crowns of the martyrs, the thrones of the apostles, and in the midst of them all she found her Son reigning. Why then does she still say: "I sought him but I did not find him?" Recall, brothers, what I said a little while ago. In that first quest of hers in which she sought him she did find him, but today she found him so perfectly, so blissfully, that she rightly confesses that previously she had not found him. Similarly, in the present instance. For she ascended higher than the highest of all the saints and came to such knowledge of the divinity that she then glories for the first time in having found him.

That is why she says: "The watchmen who guard the city found me." The "watchmen" are the angels who guard the city of God, that is, the holy Church and protect it against the snares and the attacks of the devil. And indeed, brothers, it is certain that the whole host of the angels came today to meet the most blessed Mary. They found her in the world and they bore her from the world. But although she saw the brightness of the angels and their glory and beatitude, she was not satisfied with that. Rather she desired to see him whom alone she loved above all. And therefore she says, "Have you seen him whom my soul loves?"

She adds: "Scarcely had I left them behind when I met him whom my soul loves." O blessed soul, that not only left behind the patriarchs and prophets, the apostles, martyrs, confessors and virgins but also the angels, thrones and dominations, the cherubim and seraphim and all heaven's array, and so came to her dearest Son. Then she fully found him whom now her soul loves fully. She found him and she held him. "I held him," she says, "and I will not let him go." She held him and she holds him now and she will never let him go. She holds him with the embraces of a perfect love, and she can never lose him because she can never love him any less.

Let us lift up our hearts then, brothers, to our Lady, our Advocate. Let us consider how much hope we can have in her. Just as she surpasses every creature in excellence, so also she is more merciful and benign than any creature. Let us then pray confidently to her who can assist us because of her surpassing dignity and wills to do so because of her mercy. May she implore her Son for us that as he deigned to be born of her for us, through her he may deign to have mercy on us, he who lives and reigns with the Father and the Holy Spirit through all ages of ages. Amen.

(*Sermon Twenty for the Feast of the Assumption*, 33-36)

Our Advocate

Let each one of us now consider ourselves. Let us see what sort of cause we have to present before the Lord. How have we lived in God's sight? Certainly we are humans and God is God. We are servants and God is our Lord. We are creatures and God is our Creator. We have not worshiped our God as we ought to have done; we have not obeyed our Lord as we ought to have done; we have not loved our Creator as we ought to have done. Therefore, brothers, if we consider ourselves rightly we will not be able, as the scriptures say, to answer God one question in a thousand. What then shall we do? We can hide nothing from God. For, as the apostle says, Everything lies naked and open to God's eyes. Let us offer God our prayers. Let us say to the Lord: Do not enter into judgment with your servants. It is too little, however, only to offer our own prayers. Let us seek the help of one whose prayers God will never despise. Let us approach God's Bride. Let us approach God's Mother. Let us approach God's most wonderful Handmaid. The blessed Mary is all of these.

Therefore let us celebrate with gladness the birthday of the blessed Mary in order that she may intercede for us to the Lord our God. If we have done any good by the grace of God, God will not scorn it if she presents it to her Son. Without any doubt she will obtain pardon for the evil we have done. What is then most assuredly necessary for us is that we should so stand in her presence that she would be willing to undertake our cause. But what shall we do for her? What sort of gifts shall we offer her? Would that we could at least give her what we owe her in strict justice. We owe her honor, we owe her service, we owe her love, we owe her praise.

We owe her honor because she is the mother of our Lord. For to deny honor to the mother is clearly to dishonor the son. As scripture says: "Honor your father and mother." What then shall we say, brothers? Is she not our mother? Assuredly, brothers, she is truly our mother. For through her we were born, through her we are fed, through her we grow. Through her we were born not to the world but to God. Through her we are fed not with bodily milk but with that of which the apostle says: "I gave you milk to drink instead of solid food." Through her we grow not in physical bulk but in spiritual strength. Now let us see what sort of birth this is, what sort of milk this is, what sort of growth this is.

We were all, as you believe and know, dead, aged, in darkness and in misery. Dead, because we had lost the Lord; aged, because we were corrupt; in darkness, because we had forfeited the light of wisdom and so had wholly perished. But we were born in a much better way through Mary, the blessed one, than through Eve, for Christ was born of Mary. Our aged state was replaced by a newness of life; wholeness replaced corruption; light, darkness. Mary is our mother, the mother of our life, the mother of our wholeness, the mother of our light. The apostle says of our Lord: "God made him our wisdom, our justice, our sanctification and our redemption." She, therefore, who is the mother of Christ is the mother of our wisdom, the mother of our justice, the mother of our sanctification, the mother of our redemption. So she is more a mother to us than the mother of our flesh. From her we receive a better birth, a birth to newness of life, to holiness, to wisdom, to justice, to sanctification, to redemption. Therefore with joy let us celebrate the birthday of her from whom we are so well born.

Now let us see what sort of milk we have received from her. The Word of God, the Son of God, the Wisdom of God, is bread and he is solid food. Therefore only those who were strong, the angels, ate of him. We who were little were not able to taste this food because it was solid. We who were on earth were not able to get to this bread, because it was in heaven. What happened then? This bread entered into the womb of the Blessed Virgin and there it became milk. What kind of milk? Milk such as we have been able to suck. Ponder now the Son of God on the Virgin's lap, in the Virgin's arms, at the Virgin's breast. All of this is milk, drink it in. This is the milk that our good mother provides for us. Also ponder now her chastity, her charity, her humility and by her example grow in purity, grow in charity, grow in humility and in this way follow your mother. This is how she is our mother. Therefore we ought to honor her. For this is the Lord's commandment, as we said: "Honor your father and mother."

We also owe her service because she is our Lady. For the bride of our Lord is our Lady, the bride of our King is our Queen. Therefore let us serve her. For the apostle bids us: "Servants be subject to your lords with all due fear." If those who do not serve their worldly masters violate the command of the Lord, without doubt those who do not serve their heavenly Lady are totally reprehensible. But how should we serve her? Brothers, no service pleases her as much as when with a fully affectionate love we humbly submit ourselves to her Son, because all the praise and all the service that we show to her Son she reckons as paid to herself. Let no one say: Although I do this or that against the Lord it does not trouble me; I will serve Saint Mary and thus I shall be safe. That is not so. As soon as one offends the Son that one without doubt offends the Mother also. But when we wish to be reconciled to our Lord after our sins, then it is we must seek her out and entrust our cause to her.

Again, we owe her love. For she is of our flesh and she is our sister. Do not let what I say seem overbold to you. The very Son of God because he is the Son of Man is our brother. But he derives his humanity only from his mother while she derives hers from both father and mother. See now how much we may count on her because she is our sister. Let us love her for she does indeed love us. Truly we must love this sister whose holiness, whose kindness, whose purity has been of advantage not only to herself but to all of us.

Again, we owe her praise. For scripture says: "Praise the Lord in his saints." If our Lord is to be praised in the saints through whom the Lord works wondrous deeds, how much more is the Lord not to be praised in her in whom God made himself, a wonder surpassing all wonders! If those who resolve to preserve their chastity are to be praised, how is she to be praised who, without any example, chose to preserve her virginity and yet together with virginity obtained fecundity! If those through whom God raises the dead are to be praised, how is she to be praised through whose holiness God raised the whole world from everlasting death! Therefore, brothers, let us praise her and let us celebrate with gladness the birthday of the blessed Mary in order that she may intercede for us to the Lord our God. But if we praise her with our voice let us not insult her by our behavior. Let us then not pretend to praise her but do so in very truth. To be unwilling to imitate to the best of our ability that which we praise is to praise falsely. Truly to praise the humility of Saint Mary is to do everything in our power to cultivate humility. Truly to praise her chastity is to detest and scorn all impurity and all wantonness. Truly to praise her charity is to direct all our thoughts and energies to the perfect love of God and neighbor.

(*Sermon Twenty-three for the Nativity of Saint Mary*, 4-16)

Star of the Sea

A certain star has risen for us: our Lady, Saint Mary. Her name means *star of the sea*; no doubt the star of this sea which is the world. Therefore we ought to lift up our eyes to this Star that has appeared on earth today in order that she may lead us, in order that she may enlighten us, in order that she may show us the steps so that we shall know them, in order that she may help us so that we may be able to ascend. And therefore it is a beautiful thing that Mary is placed in this stairway which we must climb. At the very moment of our conversion she appears to us and receives us into her care and enlightens us in her light and accompanies us along this laborious path.

In the first place let us see that the foundation is laid, that is, faith in Christ. For without faith it is impossible to please God. Next let us take great care always to keep before our eyes this Star which appeared on earth. Thus we shall not fail on account of the darkness of the night in which we are. And let us begin to ascend in such a way that our conversion may be perfect.

Certainly evil affections like clouds darken the soul and attempt to obscure all spiritual joy. But here especially we ought to think of that Star of ours that she may shine upon us in this night, in this darkness. . . .

This is the direct way.

(*Sermon Twenty-four for the Nativity of Saint Mary*,
20, 22, 31)

Prayer to His Healer

Look, gentle Lord, I have wandered through the world and the things in the world and know, as he who knew your secrets said, whatever exists in the world is concupiscence of the flesh or concupiscence of the eyes or pride of life. In these I sought rest for my unhappy soul, but everywhere was labor and lament, sorrow and affliction of spirit. You cried out, my Lord, you cried out and called . . . you conquered my obduracy. You sweetened, you savored, you banished my bitterness. I heard you calling but how late! Come to me, all you who labor and are heavy burdened. And I said: You will stretch your right hand to this work of your hands. I was lying rotting and covered over, bound and captive, snagged in the birdlime of clinging iniquity, overwhelmed by the weight of inveterate habits. So I interrogated myself: Who am I, where am I, what kind of person am I? I shuddered, my Lord, and trembled at my own effigy. I was terrified at the loathsome image of my unhappy soul. I was displeasing to myself, because you were becoming pleasing to me. I wanted to escape from myself and to escape into you but was paralyzed in myself. . . . The chain of my worst habits bound me, love of my kinsmen conquered me, the fetters of gracious company pressed upon me tightly; above all the knot of a certain friendship was dearer to me than all the delights of my life. I relished the others, the others were pleasing to me, but you more than any. Weighing these one by one, I recognized that sweetness was mixed with bitterness, sadness with joy, adversity with prosperity. The charming bond of friendship gratified me, though I always feared being hurt and the inevitable separation some day in the future. I pondered the joy at their beginning, I observed their progress and I foresaw their end. Now I saw that their beginnings could not escape blame nor their midpoint being offensive nor their end condemnation. The specter of death was terrifying, because after death inevitable punishment awaited such a soul. Observing certain things about me but ignorant of what was going on inside me, people kept saying: "Oh, how well things are going for him! Yes, how well!" They had no idea that things were going badly for me there where alone they could go well. Very deep within me was my wound, crucifying, terrifying and corrupting everything within me with an intolerable stench. Had you not quickly stretched out your hand to me, O Lord, unable to endure myself I might perhaps have resorted to the worst remedy of despair.

At last I began to surmise, as much as my inexperience allowed, or rather as much as you permitted, how much joy there is in your love, how much tranquillity with that joy and how much security with that tranquillity. Those who love you make no mistake in their choice, for nothing is better than you. Their hope is not cheated, since nothing is loved with greater reward. They need not fear exceeding the limit, since in loving you no limit is set. They do not dread death, the disrupter of worldly friendships, since life never dies. In loving you, they fear no offense, for none exists but the abandonment of love itself. No suspicion gets in the way, since you judge by the testimony of conscience itself. Here is joy because fear is banished. Here is tranquillity because anger is curbed. Here is security because the world is scorned.

Meanwhile, you gradually began to become tasty to my palate though it was not quite healed. And I kept saying: If only I might be healed! I was swept toward you only to fall back into myself again. Those things I used to experience pleasurably in the flesh kept me shackled, as it were, by force of habit, although what my spirit proposed by force of reason pleased me more. I often said, even in the hearing of others: Where now, I ask, are all the delights, pleasures and joys we appreciated until this very moment? Now at last, at this moment in time what sensations remain of them? Whatever was joyous has vanished. Of all these, this alone remains: what pricks our conscience, strikes the fear of death in us and condemns us to eternal punishment. I ask you, compare with all our riches, delights and honors the one joy of the servants of Christ, that they do not fear death.

In saying these words I often felt worthless and sometimes wept with bitter contrition of soul. Anything I gazed at turned worthless to me, but habits of sensual pleasure oppressed me. But you who hear the groans of the prisoners and free the children of the slain broke my chains asunder. You who offer your paradise to harlots and publicans turned me, the worst of them all, back to yourself. See, under your yoke I breathe easily and under your burden I am at rest, because your yoke is easy and your burden light.

They are wrong, O Lord, wrong and deceived who, ignorant of themselves and not recognizing what they are experiencing, complain about the harshness of your yoke and the weight of your burden. What then, you say, do you never labor, you who seem to have bowed your necks to Christ's yoke and bent your shoulders to his burden? I do, all too often. Yes, even today, I labored not a little. For when a thoughtless word escaped me a while ago, a very dear friend of mine took it so badly that he even betrayed the hurt on his face, and when I fell prostrate at his feet, he was in no hurry to lift me up. My spirit has still not sweated out that sorrow, as you know, Lord, not because I was left prostrate so long but because he was hurt and I caused this by a thoughtless word.

You forgive me for sinning because against you alone have I sinned. Yet, since I have also sinned toward my friend, I still cast myself at his feet. Please inspire him also to forgive me, because I have hurt him, although, as you know, I did not then intend nor did I wish to hurt him.

But to return to what I was saying before, does this labor of mine come from the Lord's yoke or not rather from my sickness? I sense clearly that Christ's sweet yoke gives birth to whatever tranquillity, peace and joy I have, but what labor, fatigue or lethargy I have stems from the remnant worldly concupiscence. . . . Those who dispute about the harshness of this yoke perhaps have either not completely cast off the very heavy yoke of concupiscence of the world or with greater confusion have taken up anew what was once cast off. By contrast, the Lord's yoke is easy and the Lord's burden light.

(*Mirror of Charity* 1:79-86 *passim*)

The Ointment of Consolation

Your knowledge is too excellent for me, O Lord, you are exalted far above my reach. Meanwhile, I shall embrace you, Lord Jesus. I, small, shall embrace you small; I, weak, you weak; I, a man, you, a man. For even you, O Lord, were poor, riding on a donkey, on a colt, the foal of a donkey. So I shall therefore embrace you, O Lord. All my greatness is but small to you, all my strength is weak to you, all my wisdom is foolish to you. I shall run toward the scents of your ointments, O Lord. Are you surprised that I call ointments things that heal the sick, strengthen the weak, and gladden the sorrowing? Awakened by the fragrance of your ointments and refreshed by their perfume, I shall follow you, Lord Jesus. I shall follow you, Lord, although not upon the mountains of spices where your spouse found you but in the garden where your flesh, O Lord, was sown. There you leap, here you sleep. Here, yes, here, you sleep, Lord, here you slumber, here you keep a gentle Sabbath in Sabbath rest. May my flesh be buried with you, Lord, that what I live in the flesh I may live not in myself but in you who gave yourself up for me. Let my flesh with you be anointed, O Lord, with the myrrh of modesty, that sin may no longer reign in my mortal body, that I may not become like a beast of burden rotting in its own dung.

(*Mirror of Charity* 1:22)

Return

Whence have you come into the garden? Whence, if not from the cross? If only I, too, might take up your cross, O Lord, and follow you. But how should I follow you? You ask: How did you withdraw from me? Not by the stride of my foot, I think, Lord, but by the attachment of my mind. Unwilling to keep my soul's substance for you, I took it for myself, and wishing to possess myself without you, I lost both you and myself. See what a burden I have become to myself. I became a place of gloom and misery for myself, a place of horror and a region of destitution. I shall arise, therefore, and go to my Father and say to him: Father, I have sinned against heaven and against you.

(Mirror of Charity 1:23)

The Prayer of a Puppy

Good Jesus, be present! Be present to this little pauper of yours who is not begging for the crumbs of a rich man clad in purple but, like a puppy, for those crumbs which fall from the table of my masters, your sons. That great man was your son, and because he was your son, my Lord—I mean holy Moses—he has surely been admitted to your table and has feasted on your bread in the bower of Solomon. I know, my gentle Lord, that you said, It is not fair to take the children's bread and to throw it to the dogs. But since the puppies eat the crumbs which fall from their masters' table, break some of that bread up for your puppy, so that someone who cannot manage to eat the crust may gather up the crumbs.

(Mirror of Charity 1:23)

The Field of Consolation

How often, good Jesus, does day incline to evening, how often does the daylight of some slight consolation fade before the black night of an intolerable grief? Everything turns to ashes in my mouth; wherever I look, I see a load of cares. If someone speaks to me, I barely hear; if someone knocks, I scarcely notice; my heart is turned to stone, my tongue sticks fast, my tear-ducts are dry. What then? Into the field I go to meditate. I reread the Holy Book; I set down my thoughts; and suddenly Rebecca comes running toward me and with her light, which is your grace, good Jesus, dispels the gloom, puts melancholy to flight, melts my hardness. Soon sighs give way to tears, accompanied in their turn by heavenly joy. Unhappy are those who, when oppressed in spirit, do not walk into this field and find that joy.

(Sermons on Isaiah, 27)

Prayer of the Prodigal Son

Who will grant me, good Jesus, to follow in your footsteps and so to run after you that eventually I may overtake you. I, yes I, am that prodigal son who took to himself his share of the inheritance, for I did not wish to preserve my strength for you. And set out for a distant land, the region of unlikeness, behaving as one of the dumb beasts and made like them. There I squandered all I owned in riotous living and so I began to feel want. Unhappy want, not only lacking bread but unable even to profit by the food of pigs. Following the most unclean of animals I wandered in the desert, in a waterless country, searching in vain for the way to a city I could dwell in. Hungry and thirsty, my soul wasted away in suffering. Then I said: "How many hired servants in my father's house have bread in abundance, while here I perish for hunger?" While I thus cried to the Lord he hearkened to me and led me into the right path, so that I might make my way to a city I could dwell in. What city but that which abounds in bread and is called the House of Bread, Bethlehem. May your mercies praise you, Lord, for you have filled the empty soul, and the hungry soul you have filled with good things. You have filled it with that bread indeed which came down from heaven and was laid in the manger to become the food of spiritual animals.

(Jesus at the Age of Twelve, 3)

Incarnate Majesty

O sweet Lady, with what sweetness you were inebriated, with what a fire of love you were inflamed, when you felt in your mind and in your womb the presence of majesty, when he took to himself flesh from your flesh and fashioned for himself from your members members in which all the fullness of the Godhead might dwell in bodily form. . . .

Here am I, Lord, adoring your majesty, not slaying your body, venerating your death, not mocking your passion, pondering your mercy, not despising your weakness. So may your sweet humanity intercede for me, may your unutterable loving kindness commend me to your Father. Say then, sweet Lord: "Father, forgive him. . . ."

But, sweet Jesus, why do you keep at a distance from your most sacred feet her who in her love desires to clasp them, "Do not touch me," he says. What a harsh command, now intolerable: "Do not touch me." How is this, Lord? Why may I not touch you? May I not touch, may I not kiss those lovable feet, for my sake pierced with nails and drenched in blood? Are you less gentle than usual because you are more glorious? But I will not let you go. I will not leave you. I will not spare my tears, my breast will burst with sobs and sighs unless I touch you.

(A Rule of Life for a Recluse, 29-31)

The Pastoral Prayer

O Good Shepherd Jesus,
good, gentle, tender Shepherd,
behold a shepherd, poor and pitiful,
a shepherd of your sheep indeed,
but weak and clumsy and of little use,
cries out to you.
To you, I say, Good Shepherd,
this shepherd, who is not good, makes his prayer.
He cries to you,
troubled upon his own account and troubled for your sheep.

. . .

To you, my Jesus, I confess, therefore;
to you, my Savior and my hope,
to you, my comfort and my God, I humbly own
that I am not as contrite and as fearful as I ought
to be for my past sins;
nor do I feel enough concern about my present ones.
And you, sweet Lord,
have set a man like this over your family
over the sheep of your pasture.
Me, who take all too little trouble with myself,
you bid to be concerned on their behalf;
and me, who never pray enough about my own sins,
you would have pray for them.

. . .

Did you set such a person over your household, Lord,
in order that, if it should please your goodness
to rule it well through him,
your mercy might be shown, your wisdom known,
the excellence of your power declared thereby
as yours alone, not man's;
and so the wise, the righteous, and the strong
should never glory in their wisdom,

righteousness and strength
as though they were their own;
for, when such persons rule your people well,
it is not they, but you, that rule them.
"Give not the glory unto us, O Lord, if this be so,
but unto your own name."

Yet, Lord, whatever be the reason why
you have put my unworthy, sinful self into this office,
or have suffered others to appoint me to it,
the fact remains that you command me
— so long as you allow me to hold the same —
to be concerned for those set under me,
and to pray for them most particularly.
Wherefore, O Lord,
I lay my prayers before you,
trusting not in my own righteousness,
but in your great mercy;
and where no merit of my own can lift its voice,
duty is eloquent.
Let your eyes, therefore, be upon me, Lord,
and let your ears be open to my prayers.
. . .
You know well, O Searcher of my heart,
that there is nothing in my soul that I would hide from you,
even had I the power to escape your eyes.
Woe to the souls that want to hide themselves from you.
They cannot make themselves not be seen by you,
but only miss your healing and incur your punishment.
So see me, sweet Lord, see me.
My hope, most Merciful, is in your loving kindness;
for you will see me,
either as a good physician sees, intent upon my healing,
or else as a kind master, anxious to correct,
or a forbearing father, longing to forgive.
This, then, is what I ask, O Font of pity,

trusting in your mighty mercy and merciful might:
I ask you, by the power of your most sweet name,
and by your holy manhood's mystery,
to put away my sins and heal the languors of my soul,
mindful only of your goodness, not of my ingratitude. . . .
Against these vices, Lord, may your sweet grace
afford me strength and courage;
that I may not consent thereto nor let them reign
in this my mortal body
nor yield my members to be instruments of wickedness.
And as I thus resist,
do you the while heal all my weakness perfectly,
cure all my wounds,
and put back into shape all my deformities.
Lord, may your good, sweet Spirit descend into my heart,
and fashion there a dwelling for himself,
cleansing it from all defilement both of flesh and spirit,
impouring into it the increment of faith and hope and love,
disposing it to penitence and love and gentleness. . . .
There was a wise king once, who asked
that wisdom might be given him to rule your people.
His prayer found favor in your eyes,
you did hearken thereto;
and at that time you had not met the cross,
nor shown your people that amazing love.
But now, sweet Lord, behold before your face
your own peculiar people, whose eyes are ever on your cross,
and who themselves are signed with it.
You have entrusted to your sinful servant
the task of ruling them.
My God, you know what a fool I am,
my weakness is not hidden from your sight.
Therefore, sweet Lord, I ask you not for gold,
I ask you not for silver nor for jewels
but only that you would give me wisdom
that I may know to rule your people well.

Font of wisdom, send her from your throne of might,
to be with me, to work with me,
to act in me, to speak in me,
to order all my thoughts and words and deeds and plans according to your will
and, to the glory of your name,
to further their advance and my salvation.

. . .

You know my heart, Lord.
You know that my will is that whatever
you have given your servant
should be devoted wholly to the service of your servants
and spent for them in its entirety.
And I myself, moreover, would be freely spent for them.
So may it be, O Lord, so may it be.
My powers of perception and of speech,
my work time and my leisure,
my doing and my thinking,
the times when things go well with me,
the times when they go ill,
my life, my death,
my good health and my weakness,
each single thing that makes me what I am,
the fact that I exist and think and judge,
let all be used, let all be spent for those
for whom you did deign to be spent yourself.
Teach me your servant, therefore, Lord, teach me,
I pray you, by your Holy Spirit,
how to devote myself to them
and how to spend myself on their behalf.
Give me, by your unutterable grace,
the power to bear with their shortcomings patiently,
to share their griefs in loving sympathy
and to afford them help according to their needs.
Taught by your Spirit may I learn
to comfort the sorrowful,

confirm the weak and raise the fallen;
to be myself one with them in their weakness,
one with them when they burn at causes of offence,
one in all things with them, all things to all of them,
that I may gain them all.
Give me the power to speak the truth
straightforwardly and yet acceptably
so that they all may be built up in faith and hope and love,
in chastity and lowliness, in patience and obedience,
in spiritual fervor and submissiveness of mind.
And, since you have appointed
this blind guide to lead them,
this untaught man to teach, this ignorant one to rule them,
for their sakes, Lord, if not for mine,
teach him whom you have made to be their teacher,
lead him whom you have bidden to lead them,
rule him who is their ruler.
Teach me, therefore, sweet Lord,
how to restrain the restless, comfort the discouraged,
and support the weak.
Teach me to suit myself to everyone
according to each one's nature, character and disposition,
according to each one's power of understanding or lack of it,
as time and place require, in each case,
as you would have me do.
And since the weakness of my flesh
— or it may be my lack of courage
and my heart's corruption —
prevent my edifying them by labors of watching and fasting,
I beg your bounteous mercy that they may be edified by
my humility and charity, my patience and my pity.
May my words and teaching build them up
and may they always be assisted by my prayers.
. . .
Inspire them, O Lord, also to have of me,
who am your servant, and their servant for your sake,

such an opinion as may profit them,
such love and fear of me,
as you, Lord, see to be good for them.
I, for my part, commit them
into your holy hands and loving providence.
May no one snatch them from your hand
nor from your servant's,
unto whom you have committed them.
May they persevere with gladness in their holy purpose
unto the attainment of everlasting life
with you, our most sweet Lord, their helper always,
who lives and reigns to ages of ages. Amen.

His Word and His Life in Liturgy

Aelred, as all his brother-monks, had committed himself to living according to Saint Benedict's *Rule for Monasteries.* In his *Rule*, Benedict gave pride of place to what he called "The Work of God," that is, the liturgical offices. On the great feasts, Aelred as abbot was required by Cistercian usage to gather the whole community and through a sermon help them enter more fully into the life of Christ, the whole Christ, as he is to be lived out by all Christians through the liturgical year. Scripture plays a special role in the unfolding of the liturgy, so the abbot explored especially the diverse meanings of the Sacred Text and then the mysteries of Christ as they are found therein.

It was in the course of his sermons that Aelred set forth his very rich, personalistic Christology. Certainly there is nothing abstract about it. It is very warm and affectionate. He spoke with equal warmth of the holy Mother of God, Mary. In these sermons we also find his ecclesiology and sacramentology along with his monastic theology.

Aelred here frequently addresses his "dear brothers."

That is not surprising, for these sermons represent the talks he gave to his monks in their monastery. But these sermons' fundamental Christian teaching can be fruitful for everyone baptized into Christ, man or woman.

The Teaching of Jesus
is Found in Holy Scripture

This is the teaching of Jesus which is found in holy scripture, which that Spirit has written who goes with such silence that "you know not whence he comes or whither he goes." Not thus, not thus the rivers of Egypt, the rivers of Assyria that go with a rush in the wisdom of words that make void the cross of Christ. All that learning consists in bandying with words and empty eloquence, blinding rather than enlightening minds with the sophisms of different schools of thought. Your teaching, my good Jesus, is not like that; your waters go with silence. For your teaching, Lord, does not fill the ear with fine-sounding words but is breathed into the mind by your gentle Spirit. Of you it is written. "He shall not contend nor cry out; neither shall any man hear his voice in the streets." So it is heard interiorly, heard in the heart, heard with silence.

(Sermon to the Synod)

The Consolation of the Scriptures

So, brothers, to the extent that outward persecution or inward confusion makes us sad, the divine consolation of holy scripture makes us happy. "For whatever things were written, were written for our learning; that through patience and the comfort of the scriptures we might have hope." I tell you, brothers, nothing contrary can happen, nothing sad or bitter occur, which does not either quickly go or prove more easy to bear as soon as the Sacred Page explains it to us. This is the field into which the holy Isaac went forth to meditate, the day being now well spent, where Rebecca coming to meet him softened with her gentleness the affliction that was his. How often, my good Jesus, the day draws toward evening; how often to the daylight of some little consolation the dark night of some insupportable sadness succeeds. All is turned to weariness; everything I see a burden. If someone speaks, I scarcely hear; if someone knocks, I am hardly aware of it. My heart is hardened like a stone. I cannot speak. My eyes are dry. What then? I go forth to meditate in the field. I open the Holy Book and write my thoughts on the tablets when suddenly your grace, good Jesus, like Rebecca running up, disperses the darkness with its light, drives away weariness, breaks my hardness. Soon tears succeed to sighs and heavenly joy comes with tears. Unfortunate are those who, when some sadness troubles them, do not go out into this field that they may be happy.

(Sermon Twenty-seven on the Burdens of Isaiah)

Senses of Scripture

You know that the wheel that Ezekiel saw had four faces. That wheel signifies the holy scripture. Whence the psalmist says: "Your voice resounds in a wheel." This wheel has four faces, and sometimes we consider only one of its faces, sometime two, sometimes three and sometimes even all four. Its first face is history, the second morality, the third allegory, the fourth anagogy, that is, a sense of what is above. To those who cannot grasp the deeper things, scripture shows its first face that is only simple history. And they delight in the beauty of this face. It also happens that some see only this face of scripture which in some parts is not so beautiful—as when the patriarch Juda slept with his daughter-in-law or when David, having killed Uria, took the man's wife. When they cannot see another face of scripture which is beautiful, because they saw this one face, they have despised it.

Therefore, brothers, we have heard the gospel and have considered its one face, the simple story, and it appears to us as sufficiently beautiful. For what scripture is more beautiful than this which tells of the glory of our most sweet Lord and the devotion of a faithful people? . . .

Jesus approached Jerusalem. You know, brothers, that literally Jerusalem is that city which Saint David acquired and built and in which Solomon constructed that wondrous temple of which you have often heard. . . . It is necessary that we turn our attention to another face of this scripture. Jerusalem, as you have been accustomed to hear, is interpreted as the *vision of peace*. This name first of all belongs to those who abide in the perfect vision of God, who is true peace and true tranquillity of mind, and through this enjoy in themselves true peace and tranquillity. This is that blessed company of angels, which indeed is called Jerusalem. And rightly so according to what the apostle Paul says: "The Jerusalem, which is above, is free; it is our mother." But how is Jesus said to approach this city, since he was always in it and that city never departed from him? This is that other face of scripture, anagogy, a sense of what is above.

Let us see now that face which we call allegory. According to this sense Jerusalem signifies the holy Church as it exists in men and women, to which Isaiah says: "Arise, be illumined, Jerusalem, because your light has come." The Church is called Jerusalem, not because it perfectly sees that peace which the angels see, but because it is directed toward it by believing rightly, acting well and loving fervently him who is our peace, our Lord Jesus.

(Sermon Two for the Coming of Christ, 2-9)

The Liturgical Celebration

My brothers, if we are not adequate to speak of one of God's saints and proclaim that saint's glory, how can we give a sermon on all of them? It is all the more necessary then that we should be persons of such merit that we might come to share their glory. What then must we do? How can we reach these heights? Let us listen, brothers, to some wholesome advice.

You know how throughout the entire world today everyone is praising God's saints: the angels and archangels, the apostles, martyrs, confessors and virgins. In their honor today in our holy Church there are songs, hymns, lights and all the rest that goes with a feast. The songs are a symbol of the unending celebration in which the saints live because of the ineffable joy which is theirs in God; the hymns, a symbol of the indescribable praise which they are always giving to God. Thus the psalmist says: "Blessed are those who dwell in your house, Lord; they will praise you through ages of ages." The lights signify the everlasting light in which God's saints live. That is why you sang last night: Around you, Lord, is a light that will never fail, where the souls of the saints find rest. Now, brothers, think, if you can, how exalted they are in heaven who can be exalted and honored in this way on earth. Certainly, brothers, if we could see at the same time all the glory of the world and all the praise of the world and all the joy of the world, in comparison with this joy of the saints it is nothing but absolute misery.

Therefore, brothers, you ought to know that we celebrate these feasts with lights, canticles and the like for only two reasons. These things do not profit God's saints. They derive no pleasure from this earthly singing. Their praise is Christ and he is their light, he who enlightens every human coming into this world. The first reason for these things is that by these reminders we can rouse ourselves to greater devotion. The second is because of the symbolism of which we have already spoken. We ought, then, to do as much as is required by these two reasons.

(Sermon Twenty-five for the Feast of All Saints, 1-4)

The Liturgical Year

When Jesus, our Lord and Savior, left us corporeally, he promised us the presence of his divinity, the presence of his grace: "Behold, I am with you all days until the consummation of the world." But because it is expedient for us always to be mindful of his benefits that he bestowed on us through his bodily presence, and because he knew that our memory is impaired by forgetfulness, our intellect by error, our zeal by cupidity, he kindly provided for us. Not only do the scriptures recount his benefits to us. These benefits are also re-presented for us by certain spiritual actions. Thus, when he gave his disciples the sacrament of his body and blood he told them: "Do this in memory of me."

It is for this reason, brothers, that these feasts have been instituted by the Church. By re-presenting now his birth, now his passion, resurrection, ascension, that wondrous devotion, that wondrous sweetness, that wondrous charity, which he showed for us in all these, will always be fresh in our memory. These feasts should also be an occasion of great growth in our faith when we hear with our ears and almost see beneath our eyes what Christ suffered for us; also what he gives us in this life and what he promises us after this life. He died for us, he forgives us our sins now, he promises us eternal happiness after this life.

(Sermon Nine for the Feast of the Annunciation
of the Lord, 1-2)

From Fear to Gladness

Before this day the human person had no secure grounds for rejoicing except to the extent that he knew or believed this day would come. But today you are told: Be not afraid, but love. Be not sad, but rejoice. See, here is an angel from heaven, proclaiming a great joy to you. Rejoice then on your own account and rejoice also for others, since this joy is not only for you but for the whole people. "Behold," the angel says, "I announce to you a great joy, which will be for all the people." Oh, what a joy, how great, how sweet, how desirable! Up to the present you were sad because you were dead, but now rejoice because life has come to you that you might live. You were sad because blindness had plunged you into darkness, but now rejoice, because today a light has arisen in the darkness for the upright of heart. You were sad because you were wretched, but now there has been born one who is compassionate and merciful, enabling you to enter into beatitude. You were sad because you were weighed down by the accumulation of your sins, but now rejoice because today the Savior has been born, who will save his people from their sins. This is the joy which the angle proclaims. The Savior has been born today.

Up to the present you have feared the One who created you, now love the One who will heal you. Up to the present you have feared your Judge, now love your Savior. "A Savior has been born to you today." Who is this, what is he like? Listen: "Who is Christ the Lord." The Greek word *chrisma* means "anointing" and from it is derived "Christ" which means "Anointed." That is the capacity in which our Savior comes; he comes as Christ, as the Anointed. For he is like a bridegroom coming forth from his nuptial chamber, and he has come forth anointed the better to please his bride. But with what is he anointed? Listen: "God, your God, has anointed you with the oil of gladness more than your companions. Your robes are all fragrant with myrrh and aloes and cassia."

Behold the stone which holy Jacob anointed with oil. This stone, today hewn from the mountain without human hands, that is, born of the Virgin without man's intervention, came forth anointed with the oil of exultation. And it is truly the oil of exaltation, because he has exalted like a giant to run his course. He exalted and he ran it. He showed us first in himself what he commands us to do through his apostle. The apostle says: "There should be no reluctance, no sense of compulsion, because the Lord loves a cheerful giver." So he himself, the first anointed with the oil of exaltation, entered upon the way by which he saved us not reluctantly nor under compulsion but out of his own generosity and with great exaltation. Rightly then is he called Christ, because he is anointed with the oil of gladness more than his companions. By his companions are meant all the saints who share his name, called Christians because he is called Christ. This is true also of the holy ones of the Old Testament; although they did not bear the name of Christian, they are not deprived of the reality that the name signifies. They were all anointed with the oil of gladness to which the apostle refers when he says: "Rejoicing in hope." However, since everyone finds in himself some element of sin to give grounds for sadness, he who was entirely free from sin is rightly said to be anointed with the oil of gladness more than his companions.

(*Sermon Three for the Nativity of the Lord*, 22-28)

Christ's Bodily Progress is Our Spiritual Progress

The Lord our God is one God. He cannot vary, he cannot change, as David says: "You are always the same and your years will not come to an end." Now this God of ours is eternal, outside time and unchangeable. In our nature God became changeable and entered time to make the changeableness which God took upon Godself for our sakes the way for us changeable ones, those within time. God did this so that we could enter into God's own eternity and stability. As a result in our one unique Savior there should be the way by which we might mount on high, the life to which we might come, and the truth which we might enjoy. As Christ said: "I am the way, the truth and the life."

So the Lord, without ceasing to be great in God's own nature, was born as a little child in the flesh. Through a certain interval of time the Lord advanced and grew up according to the flesh. The Lord did this in order that we who in spirit are little children, or rather almost nothing, might be born spiritually and, passing through the successive ages of the spiritual life, grow up and advance. Thus his bodily progress is our spiritual progress, and what we are told he did at each stage of his life is reproduced in us spiritually according to the various degrees of progress—as is experienced by those who advance in virtue.

(Jesus at the Age of Twelve, 11)

The Two Comings of Christ

You must know, dearest brothers, that this blessed season that we call *Adventum Domini,* Advent or the Coming of the Lord, represents two things to us. Therefore we ought to rejoice concerning both of them, for it ought to bring us a twofold benefit.

This season makes present to us both comings of our Lord. First of all, that coming in gentleness when the Son of God, the fairest of the sons of the human family, the desired of all the nations, gave to this world his visible presence in the flesh, which had been long awaited and ardently desired by all the Fathers. At that time he came into this world to save sinners. And secondly, that coming which we must expect with firm hope and, indeed, often call to mind with tears. Then this same Lord of ours, who first came hidden in the flesh, will come revealed in all glory. As is sung in the psalm: "God shall manifestly come . . . ," that is, on the day of judgment when the Lord comes openly to judge. The Lord's first coming was made known only to a few just persons. In the second coming the Lord will appear openly to just and sinners alike, as the prophet clearly implies when he says: "All flesh shall see the salvation of God." The day that we are to celebrate shortly in memory of this birth presents God to us as born, that is to say, it more precisely signifies that day and hour when God came into this world. In the same way, this season which we are observing in preparation for that day properly makes God present as longed for, that is, as the desire which the holy Fathers had, those who lived before God's coming.

Beautifully, then, is it provided in the Church that during this season the words of those who lived before the Lord's first coming are read and their longings recalled. Nor is it only for one day that we celebrate their longing but for quite a long time. This is so, for it is usual that if we are kept waiting some time for something that we much desire, when that which we love comes it seems sweeter to us. It is for us, then, dearest brothers, to follow the example of the holy Fathers and recall their longings, and thus set our minds on fire with love and desire for Christ.

You must know that it was for this reason that the observance of this season was enjoined on us: that we ought to consider the longing which the holy Fathers had for the first coming of the Lord. Through their example we learn to have a great desire for the Lord's second coming. We have to reflect what good things our Lord did for us through the first coming and that the Lord will do much greater things for us through the second. Such thoughts will lead us to a great love of that first coming and a great desire for the second. . . .

For the Lord came the first time to set us free from our sins, but in the second coming the Lord will heal all our infirmities. So it is that someone [the psalmist] bids his soul bless the Lord and he gives as his reason: "Who forgives," he says, "all your iniquities, who heals all your infirmities." The first belongs to the Lord's first coming, the second to the second. By the first coming the Lord destroyed our sins, but we still suffer great infirmities as a punishment for those sins. Who can count all the infirmities of this life: hunger, thirst, toil, pain, disease, languor, weariness? But these concern the body. How many are the infirmities of the soul! How much concupiscence, how many temptations! All these infirmities and all the others which we cannot stop to mention now the Lord will heal by the second coming. Then the apostle's words will be fulfilled: "This perishable body must be clothed in incorruptibility, etc."

(Sermon One for the Coming of the Lord, 1-5, 9)

The Approach of Love

But how does God, who is everywhere present and absent from nothing, approach this Jerusalem? God has said: "Draw close to me and I will draw close to you." How do we draw close to God, in whom we live, move and are? The prophet says: "Approach him and be enlightened." And the Lord condemned some saying: "Woe to those who have withdrawn from me." What is this approach and withdrawal? It isn't from place to place but it is from one affection to another. If you love the world, you withdraw from God. If you withdraw from love of the world and begin to love God, you then approach God. So we approach God when we grow in love of God. God approaches us when God deigns to have mercy on us.

In this way Adam withdrew from God, by loving God less and loving the world more. For he loved his own private excellence, which was not of God but of the world. In this way the whole human race withdrew from God. And therefore that which is now the Church of God withdraws from God in the same way; and so far from God that in no way can it on its own approach God or come to God. Therefore, because it could not come to God its salvation, it was necessary that God its salvation should come to it. But first God did approach. God indeed came to it when God showed that wondrous mercy by which, when hanging on the cross, the Lord poured out his blood for it. And, when his side was opened, he united the Church to himself and made it one with him, so that they might be two in one flesh. If indeed then God came to the Church, God approached it when the Lord promised mercy to it, preached that mercy and began to show it. Jesus, the salvation of the Church, the salvation for the world, the salvation of miserable humans expelled from paradise, approached Jerusalem when God foretold that God would become man and when God promised Abraham that mercy, which was later fulfilled: "In your seed all the peoples will be blessed." From the seed of Abraham, Christ would be born. Through him the curse which was brought against Adam would be abolished. Through him that blessing would be given which Isaiah foretold, saying: "And you will call your servants by another name." At first his servants were called Jews but now they are called Christians. And you will call your servants by another name, in which he who is blessed upon the earth will be blessed in the Lord. Because without doubt no one can escape damnation nor be blessed who does not have this name. . . .

But you ought to know, brothers, that he will come a second time to glorify his Church in the same form in which he came the first time to redeem it. That is what the angels told the apostles after the Lord's ascension: "He will come just as you have seen him going into heaven."

If we wish to have this peace at the Lord's second coming let us make it our aim to receive the first coming with faith and love. Let us persevere in those tasks which he showed us and taught us, nourishing in us his love and genuine desire. In that we run out to meet him as perfected humans when he comes to judge the world. He lives and reigns with the Father and the Holy Spirit, God through all ages of ages. Amen.

(*Sermon Two for the Coming of the Lord*,
10-14, 31, 38, 42)

The Eucharistic Sign

"Now this," they were told, "is your sign: You will find a baby wrapped in swaddling clothes and lying in a manger." Behold what I have said because you must love. You fear the Lord of the angels but love the little Child. You fear the Lord of majesty but love the One who is wrapped in swaddling clothes. You fear the One who reigns in heaven but love the One lying in the manger. But what does the sign which the shepherds received mean? You will find a baby wrapped in swaddling clothes and lying in a manger. It means that he is the Savior, the Christ, the Lord. But is there anything special in being wrapped in swaddling clothes and lying in a stable? Are not other children wrapped in swaddling clothes? What does this sign mean then? It means a great deal if we understand it. We do understand it if we do not merely hear these tidings but also have in our hearts the light which appeared with the angels. He appeared with light when these tidings were first proclaimed to make us realize that it is only those who have the spiritual light in their minds who truly hear.

Much can be said about this sign, but since our time is short I will say only a little and that briefly. Bethlehem, the House of Bread, is the holy Church in which the body of Christ, the true bread, is administered. What the crib is at Bethlehem, that the altar is in the Church. There are fed Christ's animals of which it is said: "Your animals shall dwell in it." This is the table of which it is written: "You have spread a table before me." In this crib is Jesus wrapped in swaddling clothes. The swaddling clothes are the sacramental veils. In this crib under the appearance of bread and wine are the true body and blood of Christ. There faith tells us Christ himself is but wrapped in swaddling clothes, that is, not visible to the eye but within the sacramental appearance. There is no greater or more evident sign of Christ's birth than that we daily receive at the holy altar his body and blood, daily see immolated for us him who was once born for us of the Virgin.

Therefore, brothers, let us hasten to the Lord's crib, but as far as we can let us first by his grace prepare ourselves to approach it. Then in the company of the angels with a pure heart, a good conscience and unfeigned faith we may sing to the Lord in the whole of our life and behavior: "Glory be to God on high and on earth peace to those of good will."

(Sermon Three for the Nativity of the Lord, 38-41)

Cause to Celebrate

Who is there who would look upon eternity making a new start, strength itself weak, bread hungry, the fountain thirsty and not be rendered dumb? Who is there who would behold the beginning of our salvation, the day of human redemption and not break forth in exultation and praise, in the sounds of feasting? God is made man. Who knows how to speak about that? Our Jesus, our Savior, our joy comes among us. Who can keep silent? If we cannot keep silent and we cannot speak, what else can we do but celebrate in song? Therefore let us celebrate God, our salvation, in song. If the angels who see God's face celebrate in song, certainly we ought not to behold God's "back" without songs of celebration. I will say more. It seems to me that in a certain sense we have a greater cause for celebrating and rejoicing than have the angels. Certainly they see God. They ponder God's wisdom, they wonder at God's power. They enjoy God's sweetness. But all of this they see in a nature other than their own. For God never took on the angelic nature. But because God became in truth an offspring of Abraham, we see our God, our Lord, our joy, in the very same nature in which we ourselves are. Therefore, brothers, in order that we might see this joy of ours, this consolation of ours, this our glory, let us pass over to Bethlehem and see this Word.

Indeed, once holy Moses said these words. "I will pass over," he said, "and see this great vision." He wished to go and see a great vision. He saw a certain bush. And in that bush there was a fire. And nonetheless, the bush did not burn. Why was that fire there? It was there to illuminate, not to consume. This was the great vision. And that was why he said: "I will pass over and see this great vision." It is as if he had read those words in the Gospel that the shepherds spoke: "Let us pass over to Bethlehem. . . ." Brothers, without doubt Moses read these words, but in the book of divine predestination where God already does what is in the future. Therefore he says: I will pass over and see this great vision.

(Sermon Three for the Nativity of the Lord, 2-4)

To See Jesus

Let us pass over to Bethlehem and see this great vision, this Word that is made. It is necessary that we pass over everything that is visible, everything that is changeable, everything that can vary this way and that, everything that can know alteration, in order that we may take our heart from everything vain and voluptuous and all that could feed it with evil pleasures. May there only be a taste for that bread which comes down from heaven and gives life to the world. Thus our mind might be made a house of bread, that is a Bethlehem. Then we will see there this Word which is made. There he will show himself to us, this fire which Moses desired to see.

The Lord will show himself to us in three ways: in this world, at the judgment and in his kingdom. In this world, as small and humble; at the judgment, as great and terrible; in the kingdom, as sweet and lovable. . . .

This was the first way in which God was shown to us: in our brokenness, in our mortality, in our weakness. Here let us see God first. Here we can all see God. No one can have any excuse. Indeed, here is a little one, so undistinguished, so weak, so poor and so totally this, that nothing is seen in him which we ought to flee. Therefore today let us pass over to Bethlehem and see. There, indeed, is a little one, so he is placed in a manger, so poor that he has not whereon to lay his head, so weak that he feeds on a mother's milk, so undistinguished that he is wrapped in swaddling clothes. Our God comes to this. This is a bending down by which God bends down so that God might raise us up not only from the sin into which we had fallen but also from the penalty of sin to which God has descended. Therefore the beginning of our salvation is there in the spectacle of God's humility. Therefore let us see our Lord first of all in this humility, in this littleness, in this poverty. And who is there who cannot see God in all these things? Now through the whole world it is known that God was made man, a little human and a poor human. But not all see God with the same eye.

Some see this and are confused. Some see this and are damned. Some see this and are consoled. And some see this to imitate it. . . .

But you who now build a Bethlehem in your own soul and pass over the lusts of the world, worldly riches and deceptive honors, you will then see Jesus, little and humble, you yourselves little and humble as you look upon his sweet face. And so you will hear his most sweet voice: "Come, blessed of my Father. Receive the kingdom, which has been prepared from the beginning of the world." Then you will enter into that kingdom and you will see Jesus, sweet and lovable. Then you will be his bride, fully prepared and decked out. Then you will be worthy of his embraces, because you will be without spot or

blemish. Then you will taste that great abundance of his sweetness, which he now pours forth into those who love perfectly
but which in this life he hides from those who fear. O my
brothers, what glory that will be, that peace, that beatitude,
that security, that joy, that sweetness, which eye has not seen
nor ear heard; it has not entered into the human heart! There
truly is Bethlehem, truly the house of bread, which will satisfy
our desire for the good when our youth will be renewed as the
eagles. Let us pass over to this Bethlehem and there see this
Word which today is made. Let us pass over, let us pass over
now in hope and desire, in love and affection. Let us see it
through a mirror, in an enigma, so that when we have passed
over what is imperfect we can see face to face our Lord Jesus
himself, who lives and reigns with the Father and the Holy
Spirit, God, through all the ages of ages. Amen.

(*Sermon Three for the Nativity of the Lord*, 8-19)

The Call

This is the Jerusalem which the Lord Jesus, who is the true
and highest peace, is building up out of living stones, the Jerusalem that aspires to the vision of him and believes most firmly
that it is to find its happiness in that vision. It is holy Church,
it is each and every holy congregation, it is each and every holy
soul. This is not new to you. "Rise up," he said, "be enlightened, Jerusalem." Rightly it is told: "Rise up," for it was lying
prostrate. Rightly it was told, "Be enlightened," for it was
blind. It was lying, blind, in the darkness, in its errors, in its
sins. Therefore it is told: "Rise up," because he who would raise
it up had already stepped down. It is told: "Be enlightened,"
because he who would enlighten it was already present. What
else does that new star proclaim from the heavens but "Rise
up, be enlightened"? The sign of the Lord's birth has appeared
in the heavens in order that we may rise from the love of

earthly things to heaven. And this sign takes the form of a star so that we may know that his birth is to bring us light.

(*Sermon Four for the Feast of the Epiphany*, 6-7)

All Points to Christ the True Light

When I consider the works of the Lord which he did when he created the world, I think of the beauty of the sun and the moon, the disposition of the stars, the depth and the breadth of the sea, the fruitfulness of the earth. All of this delights me and I say, one with the prophet: "How wonderful are your works, O Lord! In wisdom you have made them all." But this meditation and consideration does not totally seize my soul, because in all of these I do not see my Lord in his fullness. In these I can indeed see his power, his wisdom, his beauty. But I do not yet see what is more savory, more delightful. But when I turn my eyes to that work of his mercy and consider that ineffable grace by which he looked upon the wretched and because of them willed to become wretched, yes, this realization captures the whole marrow and all the bowels of my soul. And I begin to say with the prophet: "What return should I make to the Lord for all that he has given me?" Always, brothers, this sweet memory ought to be with you, but especially today when this grace of God our Savior appeared, as the apostle says: "The grace appeared. . . ." Until today, brothers, the grace of God was as it were hidden, but today it has appeared. The apostle does not say that the grace of God began but it appeared.

This grace hid in the doings of the patriarchs, the words of the prophets, in the rite of the sacrifices and in the observances of the Jews. This grace hid in the lamb of Abel, in the thigh of Abraham, in the stone of Jacob, in the tunic of Joseph, in the bush of Moses, in the rod of Aaron. For the lamb which Abel offered is the one which John pointed out today at the Jordan

River, saying: "Behold the Lamb of God, who takes away the sin of the world." He is also the God whom Abraham signified in his thigh when he spoke to his servant and said: "Place your hand under my thigh and swear to me by the God of heaven." From this thigh the flesh of Saint Mary came forth from whose flesh was born the God of heaven. He is the stone who, according to Daniel the prophet, is hewn from the mountain without hands. Jacob anointed it signifying the One of whom the psalmist said: "God, your God, has anointed you with the oil of gladness beyond all your companions." This is the fire that holy Moses saw in the bush. There are two things here: the fire and the bush. "Our God," says the apostle, "is a consuming fire." The earth, cursed in the work of Adam, brings forth thistles and thorns like a bush. This earth is human flesh. Anyone who acts in it finds only thorns, the stings and wounds of evil passions, as the apostle says: "Whoever sews in the flesh, from the flesh reaps corruption."

The true light shone forth in true flesh when today the Son of God appeared in the stuff of our mortality.

(Sermon Thirty-one for the Epiphany of the Lord, 1-5)

The Sacrament of the Eucharist

You have seen all much better and more clearly with the eyes of your heart than many saw with their bodily eyes then when it actually happened. In all these things you have tasted that the Lord is sweet. Sweet, humble, meek, merciful, kind and loving. How much sweetness he showed at that supper, which he celebrated with his disciples before his passion!

At that supper he told his disciples: I have longed with great desire to eat this passover with you before I suffer. At that supper the old Passover which the Jews were accustomed to celebrate came to an end, and the new Passover which we celebrate began. How could he have shown us greater sweetness than by leaving us as a memorial of himself his own body and blood? For it was his will that the price which he paid for us once should always be before our eyes. In the wonderful generosity of his love he wished his body and blood to be not only our ransom but also our food.

Does it not seem to you, my brothers, that he very clearly fulfilled at his supper what the prophet David said: "There is a cup in the Lord's hand of foaming wine, full of spices. He has poured it from one to another." For after he had celebrated that Passover which the Jews were accustomed to celebrate with the flesh of a lamb and blood, Jesus took bread and giving it to his disciples said: "This is my body. And afterwards he did likewise with a cup, saying, This is my blood." You see how there is a cup in the Lord's hand? What is this cup but the established usages of the Law? This cup was full of foaming wine, that is, pure wine. This wine is the spiritual meaning which was contained in those usages of the old law. It is wine because it gave joy to the heart of men and women. It is wine because it inebriated those who understood it. It inebriated them with the love of God. It inebriated them to the extent that they forgot themselves and loved God alone, desired only God. Was not David inebriated with this wine when, as if drunk, he took off his clothes, uncovered himself, to dance before the ark of the Lord? Was not Isaiah inebriated with this wine when, as he himself relates, he walked before all the people naked and barefoot?

But, although this wine was pure in itself, yet because certain carnal observances were still mixed with it, the cup in the Lord's hand of foaming wine is full of spices. Consider that lamb which at this supper our Lord held in his hands. You see there that established usage of the Law like a cup in the Lord's hand. In this cup, that is, in this usage, there was pure wine, that is, a spiritual meaning. On the other hand, you see bread and wine, as it were another cup. In this cup there was not at first that spiritual wine. Now you see how he poured the wine that was in the one cup into the other. What was the wine in the old usage? The lamb symbolized the body of Christ, the lamb's blood the blood of Christ. There you have the wine in the first cup. But he poured it from one to another. Let me tell you how. "He took bread and said: This is my body. He also took wine and said: This is my blood." There is the change. The lamb that contained in symbol Christ's body and blood is left empty. The other cup has been filled, because the bread has become the body of Christ and the wine the blood of Christ.

Let us see yet more. That lamb represented the Lord's passion. That is why the command was given that as a memorial of the Lord's passion that lamb should be slaughtered every year. The commemoration of the Lord's passion in the lamb was like the wine in the cup. But God has poured it from one into another, for he has transferred the commemoration of his passion, which was previously in that lamb, to the sacrament of his body and blood, which he has now given to his disciples, saying: "Do this in commemoration of me." Here there was a certain mixture on account of material observances, for although the lamb symbolized the body of Christ, it was not really the body of Christ but a lamb. In our sacrament there is no mixture, for after the consecration our sacrament is no longer the substance of an animal and it is not the bread and wine that it was, but it is really and truly the body and blood of Christ.

(*Sermon Eleven for the Feast of Easter,* 3-12)

The Glory of the Passion of Christ

What could the recalling of the Lord's passion effect in your hearts? What was it like to see our most sweet Lord bound, spat upon, buffeted? How Isaiah fed upon this sight—not indeed that he saw it happening, but he related it as a fact. So he said, "Many were astonished at you, so will his appearance be demeaned among men, his beauty among the sons of men."

Many indeed were astonished when he fed five thousand men with five loaves and two fishes. Many were astonished when he gave light to the man who was born blind. Many were astonished when he restored Lazarus to life. They were astonished, they praised him, they gave him glory. Great was that glory but no less was the outrage which they perpetrated on him later. That is why the prophet says: "His appearance will be demeaned among men." "Demeaned" (*inglorius*) means without glory. And his appearance was indeed without glory when his face was covered and spat upon. His beauty was without glory when they crowned him with thorns, when they scourged him and struck his head with a reed. It was without glory but, as the prophet says, among the sons of men. For among the sons of God all this outrageous treatment is great glory. To such an extent, in reality, was this all glory that the same prophet says: "We saw him and there was no beauty in him, and we desired him as a man despised." It was as such that Isaiah desired him. Why? Because he saw that all that degradation would be the salvation of the human race and the glory of Christ himself.

The apostle shows this clearly when he says: "He humbled himself, becoming obedient unto death, even death on a cross." Behold the degradation. But listen to what comes next: "Therefore God exalted him. . . ." Saint David proclaimed the same prophecy: "From the torrent beside the path he will drink, and therefore he will hold his head high." He drank from the torrent because he tasted the bitterness of this life, but it was beside the path, that is, in passing. For his sufferings were soon finished, his death was soon transformed. Therefore he held his head high. For it was because he died that he rose again, and he was glorified because he rose.

Now, what sweetness was your heart able to imbibe when with your inner eye you saw the Lord carrying his cross? Who can rightly appreciate that humility, that meekness, that patience? He was led like a sheep to the slaughter, like a lamb before its shearers he was silent and did not open his mouth. How sweet it was to behold the wounds of Christ as if in the hour he received them, to stand as it were by his cross, to see those tears of his mother, to hear that sweet voice: "Father, forgive them for they know not what they do." What hope for the forgiveness of our sins could we not conceive when we heard him praying so sweetly even for his enemies. But this sweetness was not that of milk but that of wine. For while on the one hand it was sweet, on the other hand it had a bitter quality. The sweetness lay in the affection and devotion, but at the same time a certain tender sadness and compassion lent it that biting quality. For you should not look upon those sweet hands being pierced with such hard nails without a certain sweet sadness. Similarly with the piercing of his feet by the iron and the wounding of that most tender side with the lance. Nor could you behold those most sweet tears of Our Lady without compassion, though it again was sweet.

(Sermon Eleven for the Feast of Easter, 19-25)

The Ascension of the Lord

For some time we have been keeping before our minds the resurrection of our Lord Jesus Christ, for the same length of time as he spent in the world after his resurrection. Today we recall the day on which he showed us plainly that everything which he did and suffered in this world he did to lead us from the death into which we fell through Adam to true life, and to raise us up from this exile to our homeland for which we were created, that is, to heaven.

He died for our sins and he rose for our justification and he ascended into heaven for our glorification. Through his death we received the forgiveness of our sins. For what we could not do he did in satisfaction for our sins. Through faith in this resurrection we are justified. . . . Our faith, however, merits justification and expects a great reward, because we believe what we can not see. That is why the Lord said to Thomas,

"Because you have seen me, you have believed. Blessed are they who have not seen and have believed." However, that beatitude which we expect he wished today to show forth in his own person by ascending into heaven. He did this so that we might be certain that we, who are his members, will ascend to where he who is our head has ascended.

Therefore, dearest brothers, we ought to celebrate this day with great joy, because there can be no greater glorification of the human person than that which has been shown to us today. This nature of ours, which had been so degraded and corrupted that it was even compared to brute animals—as the prophet says, "The human when in honor did not understand and became comparable to stupid beasts"—this nature was raised to such a height in our Lord Jesus Christ that the whole of creation is beneath it. Even the angels adore it as something above them.

As you have often heard, after his resurrection for forty days our Lord wished for many reasons to remain in this world in bodily form. He wished to confirm his resurrection and to show in many ways that he truly rose from the dead in the flesh. Therefore, he often ate and drank with his disciples and he openly showed them his wounds. And when the apostle Thomas did not wish to believe that the other apostles had seen him, Jesus allowed Thomas to touch his side and his hands. His disciples were grieved beyond measure during his passion and almost despaired. He wished to strengthen them by his bodily presence. He wanted to prove to them by the authority of the scriptures that it was necessary for him to die and to rise again. He opened for them the meaning of the scriptures so that they might understand them.

This, too, we should notice: Before his passion and resurrection he fasted for the same amount of time that he chose to be with his disciples in the flesh after the resurrection. By his fasting he showed us the value of the physical suffering which we must undergo in this life. By the physical presence with which he favored his own after his resurrection we are able to understand the consolation of his most sweet presence, which we will have after our own resurrection. Both were commended to us over the same length of time, because it is in the measure in which we bear affliction for Christ in this life that we shall receive consolation in the future.

So our Lord ascended to the Father today, while the disciples watched in amazement and exultation, though it was an exultation mixed with sorrow. They exulted because he in whom they had placed their hope was so powerful that by his own power he could penetrate the heavens. They exulted because they knew that they also would be where he had ascended, as he had said to the Father before his passion, "I will that where I am they too may be with me. . . ." They exulted because they were shortly to receive the Holy Spirit as Jesus had promised and by his consolation they would be strengthened against all temptations. Moreover, they exulted seeing angels clothed in white who asked them, "Men of Galilee, why stand there looking up into heaven?"

They are appropriately called Galilaeans for the name means "emigrating." It implies that they were moving away from the material observances of the Law to the things of the spirit. Before the passion they had been told by the Lord, "Do not take the road to Gentile lands and do not enter any Samaritan town but go rather to the lost sheep of the house of Israel." Now an emigration is enjoined upon them. The Lord tells them, "Go forth to the whole world and proclaim the gospel to every creature."

"Men of Galilee, why stand there looking up into heaven?" No wonder. Although they were exulting for all the reasons that I have mentioned, they felt no small grief at the departure that had just taken place. For his presence in the body was very pleasing to them. In it they took great pleasure. What had brought them such joy while they possessed it certainly could not be given up without sorrow. Therefore they did what they could. They looked up into heaven, whither he had ascended. With their eyes at least they followed him whom they loved.

The angel asked them, "Men of Galilee, why stand here looking up into heaven? This Jesus who has been taken away from you up to heaven will come in the same way as you have seen him go." There is considerable comfort here. "Will come in the same way." How? With the same flesh, with the same features, with the scars and the wounds that he took to heaven. "They will look upon him whom they pierced."

We too, dearest ones, shall see our poor Lord, whom we paupers follow, but we will see him not poor, not veiled, not hidden nor mute. Our God will come openly, our God, and our God will not be silent. . . . Let it be our sole anxiety to remain attached to him with our whole heart, our whole mind, our whole strength, remembering who is our Head, where our Head is. Let us live as befits the members of that Head with our minds fixed not here where our lower part is but there where our Head has ascended today.

(*Sermon Thirteen for the Ascension of the Lord*, 1-6, 32-38)

The Assumption of the Virgin Mother

Now, among all those who are God's, the one who tastes God's goodness more intimately and with greater enjoyment is of greater excellence, more blessed and more attractive. This one, the holy virgin Mary, is not only someone God created, a handmaid, a friend and a daughter to God but she is also God's mother. So then it is only right that we should welcome her feast with greater delight and pleasure and in its celebration allow ourselves a more abundant spiritual banquet. Indeed, brothers, we ought always to praise and honor her and with all devotion recall her sweetness. But today we should rejoice with her even more, because today her joy was brought to a complete fullness. Great was her joy when the angel greeted her. Great was her joy when she felt the coming of the Holy Spirit, when that marvelous union of the Son of God with her flesh took place in her womb, so that one and the same was the Son of God and her Son. Great was her joy when she held such a Son in her arms, when she kissed him, when she took care of him, when she listened to his talk, when she saw his miracles. And because her sorrow was so great at the passion, wondrous again was her joy at his resurrection and greater still at his ascension. But all these joys were surpassed by that which she receives today. . . .

Up to this day, brothers, Mary, the blessed mother of God, knew her dearest Son in the flesh. Although, after that dear Son and Lord of hers ascended into heaven, she centered all her desires and all her love where he was. As long as she remained in this corruptible flesh, her memory could not cease to recall what she had seen of him in the flesh. For his deeds and his words were always coming to mind, and above all the features of his beautiful face were constantly in her heart. Today, however, she passed from this world and went up to the heavenly kingdom. There she began to contemplate his brightness, power and divinity, and her joy and her yearning were fulfilled. So with good reason she could say: "I have found him whom my soul loves." She holds him and she does not let him go.

(*Sermon Twenty for the Assumption of Saint Mary*,
2-3, 5-6)

Words on Friendship

Since the earliest days of Christian asceticism, when a beginner or a disciple approached a spiritual father or mother, they would humbly ask for "a word of life." The pithy response from the wise one would often serve the disciple for many weeks and even months. As the "word" was repeated again and again, under the influence of the Spirit and in response to an ardent prayerful desire, it would gradually reveal its fuller significance and open the way into a deeper and deeper understanding. However, it would not just form the mind. It would bring the mind down into the heart and form the whole of the person until the "word" became the wisdom of the disciple.

Aelred has sprinkled through his treatises many such "words of life." Here we gather but a few of them relative to his way of friendship. Abiding with them, or rather letting them, one by one, abide with us, will lead us into a fuller understanding of the way of friendship. And if we will allow it, the "word" will even form our hearts, leading us into an actual living of this sure way into divine union.

Words on Friendship

Since that sweet name of Christ has claimed my affection for itself, whatever I henceforth read or hear, though it be treated ever so subtly and eloquently, will have no relish or enlightenment for me if it lacks the salt of the heavenly books and the flavoring of that most sweet name.

(*Spiritual Friendship* 1:8)

What more sublime can be said of friendship, what more true, what more profitable than that it ought to and is proved to begin in Christ, continue in Christ, and be perfected in Christ?

(*Spiritual Friendship* 1:10)

Since in friendship eternity blossoms, truth shines forth, and charity grows sweet, consider whether you ought to separate the name of wisdom from these three?

(*Spiritual Friendship* 1:68)

In human affairs nothing more sacred is striven for, nothing more useful is sought after, nothing more difficult is discovered, nothing more sweet experienced and nothing more profitable possessed, for friendship bears fruit in this life and in the next.

(*Spiritual Friendship* 2:9)

We would be compared to a beast if we had no one to rejoice with us in adversity, no one to whom to unburden our mind as sorrow crosses our path or with whom we can share our moments of sublimity and illumination.

(Spiritual Friendship 2:10)

The best medicine in life is a friend.

(Spiritual Friendship 2:13)

Among the stages leading to perfection, friendship is the highest.

(Spiritual Friendship 2:15)

Friendship can begin among the good, progress among the better, and be consummated among the perfect.

(Spiritual Friendship 2:38)

I would say that those are beasts rather than humans who declare that one ought to live in such a way as to be to no one a source of consolation, to no one a source even of grief or burden, to take no delight in the good fortune of another or impart to others no bitterness because of their own misfortune, caring to cherish no one and to be cherished by no one.

(Spiritual Friendship 2:52)

A truly loyal friend sees nothing in his friend but his heart.

(Spiritual Friendship 3:62)

Without friends absolutely no life can be happy.

(Spiritual Friendship 3:76)

It is a law of friendship that a superior should be on a plain of equality with an inferior.

(Spiritual Friendship 3:90)

In friendship, which is the perfect gift of nature and grace alike, let the lofty descend, the lowly ascend, the rich be in want, the poor become rich.

(*Spiritual Friendship* 3:91)

Since you and your friend should be of one heart and one soul, it is unjust if there is not also but one purse.

(*Spiritual Friendship* 3:99)

We would lead a very happy life if these two words were taken from our midst: "mine" and "yours."

(*Spiritual Friendship* 3:101)

The best companion of friendship is reverence, so the one who deprives friendship of respect takes away its greatest adornment.

(*Spiritual Friendship* 3:102)

A friend's power in counseling needs be great, since there can be neither doubt of loyalty nor suspicion of flattery.

(*Spiritual Friendship* 3:103)

If our ears are so closed to the truth that we are not able to hear the truth from a friend, our salvation must be despaired of.

(*Spiritual Friendship* 3:105)

The wounds inflicted by a friend are more tolerable than the kisses of flatterers.

(*Spiritual Friendship* 3:105)

For this is well-ordered friendship: That reason rules affection and we attend more to the general welfare than to our friend's good humor.

(Spiritual Friendship 3:118)

For this is rightly ordered affection: not to love what is not to be loved; to love what is to be loved but not to love in a greater measure than is due; not to love with equal affection those who should be loved with different degrees nor to love in different measure those who should be equally loved.

(Mirror of Charity 3:18)

Who of us, if we do not love ourselves, can love our neighbor, for as we love ourselves so are we to love our neighbor.

(Spiritual Friendship 3:128)

For the one who speaks ought not only consider what he experiences within himself but also what others can experience within themselves. For one will willingly listen when what he hears from another he finds within himself.

(Sermon Thirty-three for the Purification of Saint Mary, 5)

Chronology

1110	Born at Hexham in Northumberland
c1124	Entered the court of David I of Scotland
c1130	Appointed *Dispensator*
1134	Entered Rievaulx
1138	At his father's death bed with his two brothers
1142	Journeyed to Rome, stopping at Clairvaux
	Appointed Novice Master, began the *Mirror of Charity* (probably completed at Revesby)*
1143	Founding Abbot of Revesby in Lincolnshire
1147	Elected third abbot Rievaulx

Intervening years:

Began *Spiritual Friendship*

On Jesus at the Age of Twelve

A Rule of Life for a Recluse

Life of Saint Ninian

Genealogy of the Kings

Battle of the Standard

Life of King Edward the Confessor (c1154)

On the Burdens of Isaiah

Completed *Spiritual Friendship* (c1166)

Dialogue on the Soul (c1166)

1159	Papal schism, Aelred stands with Alexander III
1167	January 12, Aelred dies at Rievaulx.
1476	Feast promulgated by the Cistercian Order

*It is not possible to date any of Aelred's writings with absolute surety.

Select Bibliography

Aelred of Rievaulx, *The Works of Aelred of Rievaulx,* Cistercian Fathers Series (Spencer. MA: Cistercian Publications, 1971—).

_____. *Dialogue on the Soul,* tr. C. H. Talbot, Cistercian Fathers 22 (Kalamazoo, MI: Cistercian Publications, 1981).

_____. *Jesus at the Age of Twelve,* tr. Theodore Berkeley, Cistercian Fathers 2 (Spencer, MA: Cistercian Publications, 1971) pp. 3-39.

_____. *The Life of Ninian* in *Vita Niniani Pictorum Australium apostoli,* ed. and tr. Alexander Penrose, The Historians of Scotland 5 (Edinburgh: Edmonston and Douglas, 1874). pp. 3-26.

_____. *The Life of Saint Edward, King and Confessor,* tr. Jerome Bertram (Guildford: St. Edward's Press, 1990).

_____. *Liturgical Sermons* I, tr. Theodore Berkeley and M. Basil Pennington, Cistercian Fathers 55 (Kalamazoo, MI: Cistercian Publications, 2000).

_____. *The Mirror of Charity,* tr. Elizabeth Connor, Cistercian Fathers 17 (Kalamazoo, MI: Cistercian Publications, 1990).

_____. *The Pastoral Prayer,* tr. R. Penelope Lawson, Cistercian Fathers 2 (Spencer, MA: Cistercian Publication, 1971) pp. 105-118.

_____. *A Rule of Life for a Recluse,* tr. Mary Paul Macpherson, Cistercian Fathers 2 (Spencer, MA: Cistercian Publications, 1971), pp. 41-102.

_____. *Spiritual Friendship,* tr. Mary Eugenia Laker, Cistercian Fathers 5 (Washington, DC: Cistercian Publications, 1974); tr. Mark F. Williams (Scranton: Scranton University Press, 1994).

Bouyer, Louis, *The Cistercian Heritage,* tr. Elizabeth A. Livingston (London: Mowbray, 1958).

Brooke, Odo, "Monastic Theology and St. Aelred" in *Studies in Monastic Theology,* ed. M. Basil Pennington, Cistercian Studies 37 (Kalamazoo, MI: Cistercian Publications, 1980) pp. 219-225.

Connor, Elizabeth, "The Doctrine of Charity in Book One of Aelred of Rievaulx's *The Mirror of Charity*" in *Cistercian Studies Quarterly* 29 (1994) 61-82.

_____. "Monastic Profession According to Aelred of Rievaulx" in *Studiosorum Speculum: Studies in Honor of Louis J. Lekai, O. Cist.,* edd. Francis R. Swietek and John R. Sommerfeldt, Cistercian Studies 141 (Kalamazoo, MI: Cistercian Pulbications, 1993) pp. 63-73.

_____. "Saint Bernard's Three Steps of Truth and Saint Aelred of Rievaulx's Three Loves" in *Bernardus Magister,* Cistercian Studies 135 (Kalamazoo, MI: Cistercian Publications, 1992) pp. 225-238.

Constable, Giles, "Aelred of Rievaulx and the Nun of Watton" in *Monks, Hermits and Crusaders in Medieval Europe* (Brookfield, VT: Variorum, 1988).

Costello, Hilary, "Hesychasm in the English Cistercians of the Twelfth and Thirteenth Centuries" in *One Yet Two. Monastic Tradition East and West,* ed. M. Basil Pennington, Cistercian Studies 29 (Kalamazoo, MI: Cistercian Publications, 1976) pp. 332-351.

Diemer, Paul, "The Witness of the Early English Cistercians to the Spirit and Aims of the Founders of the Order of Citeaux" in *The Cistercian Spirit,* ed. M. Basil Pennington, Cistercian Studies 3 (Spencer, MA: Cistercian Publications, 1970) pp. 144-165.

Dumont, Charles, "Aelred of Rievaulx's *Spiritual Friendship*" in *Cistercian Ideals and Reality,* ed. John R. Sommerfeldt, Cistercian Studies 60 (Kalamazoo, MI: Cistercian Publications, 1978) pp. 187-198.

_____. "Seeking God in Community According to St. Aelred" in *Contemplative Community,* ed. M. Basil Pennington, Cistercian Studies 21 (Washington, DC: Cistercian Publications, 1972) pp. 115-149.

_____. "Personalism in the Community According to Aelred of Rievaulx" in *Cistercian Studies Quarterly* 12 (1977) 250-271.

Dutton, Marsha L., "Christ, Our Mother" in *Goad and Nail,* ed. E. Rozanne Elder, Cistercian Studies 84 (Kalamazoo, MI: Cistercian Publications, 1985) pp. 21-45.

_____. "The Face and Feet of Christ in Bernard of Clairvaux and Aelred of Rievaulx" in *Bernardus Magister,* ed. John R. Sommerfeldt, Cistercian Studies 135 (Kalamazoo, MI: Cistercian Publications, 1992) pp. 202-223.

_____. "A Prodigal Writes Home: Aelred of Rievaulx's *De institutione inclusarum*" in *Heaven on Earth,* ed. E. Rozanne Elder, Cistercian Studies 68 (Kalamazoo, MI: Cistercian Publications, 1983) pp. 35-42.

Gilson, Etienne, *The Mystical Theology of Saint Bernard,* tr. A.H.C. Downes, Cistercian Studies 120 (Kalamazoo, MI: Cistercian Publications, 1990).

Glidden, Aelred, "Aelred the Historian: The Account of the Battle of the Standard" in *Erudition at God's Service,* ed. John R. Sommerfeldt, Cistercian Studies 98 (Kalamazoo, MI: Cistercian Publications, 1987) pp. 175-184.

Hallier, Amedee, *The Monastic Theology of Aelred of Rievaulx,* tr. Columban Heaney, Cistercian Studies 2 (Kalamazoo, MI: Cistercian Publications, 1969).

Heaney. Columban, "Aelred of Rievaulx: His Relevance to the Post-Vatican II Age" in *The Cistercian Spirit.* Ed. M. Basil Pennington, Cistercian Studies 3 (Spencer, MA: Cistercian Publications, 1970) pp. 166-189.

McGuire, Brian Patrick, *Brother and Lover: Aelred of Rievaulx* (New York: Crossroad, 1994).

Merton, Thomas, "St. Aelred of Rievaulx and the Cistercians" in *Cistercian Studies* 20 (1985) 212-223; 21 (1986) 30-42; 22 (1987) 55-75; 23 (1988) 45-62; 24 (1989) 50-68.

Pennington, M. Basil, *The Last of the Fathers: The Cistercian Fathers of the Twelfth Century* (Still River, MA: St. Bede's Publications, 1983).

_____. "The Mirror of Charity" in *Christian Spirituality: The Essential Guide to the Most Influential Spiritual Writings of the Christian Tradition,* edd. Frank N. Magill and Ian P. McGreal (San Francisco: Harper & Row, 1988) pp. 110-116.

Squire, Aelred, *Aelred of Rievaulx,* Cistercian Studies 50 (Kalamazoo, MI: Cistercian Publications, 1981).

Walter Daniel, *The Life of Aelred of Rievaulx,* tr. F. M. Powicke, Cistercian Fathers 57 (Kalamazoo, MI: Cistercian Publications, 1994).

Aelred Web Page:
http://www.une.edu.au/campus/st-alberts/aelred.htm